MUSIC IS FOREVER

Dizzy Gillespie, the Jazz Legend, and Me

Dave Usher
with
Berl Falbaum

Certificate of Registration
Registration Number: TXu-1-870-525
Effective Date of Registration: May 1, 2013

ISBN-978-0-692-21110-6 (softcover)
ISBN-978-0-692-21113-3 (eBook)

Printed in the United States

First Edition, 2014

Published by:

Red Anchor Productions (RAP)
Detroit, MI 48209

Dedication

To those who are prepared

to open their hearts and minds

to different art forms so that we

might broaden our understanding

of each other.

About the Cover

The title of this book is based on a song, "Music Is Forever," written by Annie Ross, jazz vocalist, lyricist, and accomplished actress, with Russ Freeman, jazz pianist. Ross, a member of the famous vocal trio, Lambert, Hendricks & Ross, also wrote "Twisted," enjoyed an international reputation and is a legend in jazz history. Ross said "Music Is Forever" was a love song to musicians, and I agreed when I decided to use the song's title for this book. Recalling many of jazz's greatest artists, she sings, "They say that nothing is forever but, then again, what do they know...when they say nothing is forever, nothing is forever, I just smile cause I know it's not true...music is forever. You still live when we listen to you."

When she mentions Dizzy Gillespie specifically, Ross sings, "Dizzy, oh Dizzy, oh Dizzy...oh Diz... you still live when we listen to you...they say you're gone but I don't have to believe it if I don't want to."

Ross performed the song with Mike Longo's 18-piece New York State of the Art Jazz Ensemble in the John Birks Gillespie Auditorium in New York's Bahá'i Center on October 24, 2009 to celebrate what would have been Dizzy's 92nd birthday. (Dizzy, who was born on October 21, 1917, died at 75 in 1993.) Longo, jazz pianist, played with Dizzy for 24 years.

The photo on the cover of Dizzy, with camera in hand, and me, was taken in 1987 in Nice, France where Dizzy performed in a jazz festival. The trip had a second objective: Dizzy had bought a piece of land in Saint-Paul-de-Vence between Nice and Cannes on which he planned to build a house. We went to visit the site to see if I would buy a lot next to his so we might live side-by-side in retirement. I never bought any land, and Dizzy died when he was still going strong and before he had a chance to retire.

On Music, Jazz and the Blues. . .

Men have died for this music. You can't get more serious than that.

It's taken me all my life to learn what not to play.

I don't care much about music. What I like is sounds.

*I don't think there is a definition of the blues or jazz.
I haven't heard anyone define it yet. It's indefinable.*

*Jazz music is a special language that transcends national languages
in the form of phrasing...the form of phrasing is a language all in itself...*

John Birks "Dizzy" Gillespie

Table of Contents

Introduction

by
Berl Falbaum

I first met Dave Usher sometime in 1991, and that meeting resulted from circumstances that occurred about two or three years earlier.

I was vice president of communications for a Detroit-based company and had written a letter to the editor of a business journal, lambasting its irresponsible coverage of my employer. Dave read the letter and when he met the chairman of the company I was working for at a social event, Dave told my boss that he was impressed. He wondered if I would do some work for him. Of course, that was impossible since I had a full-time job.

However, after I resigned from that position and founded my own PR company in 1989, I included Dave on a list of potential clients that I intended to contact. I wanted to pursue the possibility that he might still be interested in PR work. I asked the chairman if he remembered the name of Dave's company, but he didn't. My research — checking all the phone books in the area searching for a company whose name might begin with "Usher"— proved futile. Regretfully, I ended my search. *C'est la vie.*

As luck would have it, one day I was reading the business section of a local paper and saw a photo of Dave Usher and a story about his company, Marine Pollution Control (MPC), which he founded.

I wrote Dave a letter, outlining what my former employer had told me, and Dave responded by inviting me to lunch. We ate, we talked — for about two

i

to three hours — and, as they say, the rest is history. I was hired to assist with PR for MPC and the Spill Control Association of America (SCAA) which Dave also founded and was president of for many years.

Our relationship quickly developed into one of total mutual trust and respect, and, in fact, into a close personal friendship. Dave, I discovered, was a *mensch*, a Jewish word meaning that the individual has a heart and soul, and he/she is a person of honor and integrity. If anyone ever fit all the nuances of that word, it was Dave.

I learned that while demonstrating a tough and rough exterior, frequently coloring his language with profanity, he was actually a softy. He had a big heart and suffered fools too long, both in his professional and personal relationships. He just couldn't seem to cut ties even when warranted and well overdue. And I know he knows, though he may not admit it, he has paid a price for his humanity.

As I carried out my PR responsibilities for MPC, I discovered Dave's history with Dizzy Gillespie and the world of jazz. He told fascinating stories although he told them very matter-of-factly. There was no bragging, but just a recounting of his years in jazz, and his friendship with Dizzy which he valued immensely. It is no exaggeration to indicate he considered Dizzy a brother, as Dave states frequently in this book.

On one occasion, when Dizzy was in Detroit and stayed at Dave's apartment, I met the jazz giant and exchanged a few pleasantries with him. I was tempted to ask him to play a few bars. I was confident Dizzy would have done so, but I didn't ask, believing it would be an imposition.

Listening to Dave's stories, I recognized that he was a part of music history, important history that needed to be documented and saved. Here was a white Jew from the North and a black man from the South who practiced the Bahá'i Faith, partnering to develop and promote jazz. And it was not just with Dizzy. Because of his relationship with Dizzy, Dave met, worked with and befriended some of this country's most outstanding jazz musicians: John "Trane" Coltrane, Ahmad Jamal, Baron "Toots" Thielemans, Ramsey Lewis,

Kenny Clarke, Charlie "Yardbird" Parker, Annie Ross, The Jones Brothers, Yusef Lateef, and many others. I was in awe and a little jealous.

Moreover, this partnership with Dizzy began in 1944, at a time when race was still an incendiary issue. The South remained segregated; *Brown v. Board of Education* which would hold that separate educational facilities were inherently unequal, would not be handed down by the U.S. Supreme Court for another 10 years. Even after the Supreme Court ruling, Southern governors continued to defy court orders and the federal government to integrate schools, and lynching in the South was not yet a matter of history.

It is true that black musicians had "relationships" with record companies run by whites and with white agents, but these, as Dave indicates in his story, were, at times, tinged with distrust. Black artists knew that some white executives in the music business were exploiting them. With limited opportunities, if black musicians wanted increased exposure for their music they had no choice but to accept contracts and financial offers that were not always fair.

The Dizzy-Dave relationship piqued my curiosity. How did they meet? How was this Gillespie-Usher partnership born? Did they discuss the racial implications of their friendship? Did they consider that they might not be accepted? Was there resentment from white and/or black musicians? What was it like to work with Dizzy and the other world-class artists? I had so many questions, questions I believed Dave needed to answer not to satisfy my curiosity, but to satisfy history.

So I asked Dave whether he would be interested in working on a book on his Dizzy/jazz experiences. I argued that this history needed to be saved. He had a unique story that deserved and had to be recorded for millions of jazz fans, and future generations. I implied, subtly, that he almost had an obligation to do so. Dave reacted passively. "Yes," he said, "it sounds like a good idea. Maybe you're right. I'll sleep on it."

After I worked for Dave for about two years, he faced financial pressures at MPC, and told me he could no longer afford PR and ended our professional relationship. It was evident in his voice that it hurt him to do so. He felt bad for me, and he kept apologizing. I told him I understood and respected his decision. We maintained our friendship, and had lunch two, three times a year, as I did with Dave's son, Charlie, who became president of MPC in 2004. Dave and I called each other on Rosh Hashanah (the Jewish New Year) and Yom Kippur (the Day of Atonement) wishing each other a *gut yontiff* (good holiday.)

The years passed, but he never raised the subject of the book, although I would revisit the issue with him periodically. The answer was always the same: "I'll think about it, sleep on it." And that he did for some 20 years.

I had given up until after I published a mobster thriller in December 2011. I was quasi-retired and found myself with time on my hands. I decided to call Dave and ask him again. This time his response was a bit more positive. I sensed a different tone in his voice. He listened more closely. I said I didn't need a decision during the phone conversation, but that I would call back in a few days (Dave, at 82 at the time, couldn't wait another 20 years, and I, at 73, couldn't either) and when I did call, it was apparent he had more interest than he'd had years earlier. Actually, he said, "Yes, let's do it."

I set up an appointment at his apartment by the Detroit River just west of downtown Detroit at which I outlined the entire process — the interviews, how much time I would need, my time commitments in writing a draft, reviewing drafts, legal considerations, searching for a publisher, marketing. At the same session, I spent more than two hours delving into his family history.

That was the first of many interviews, all of which I tape-recorded. I interviewed him over a seven-month period. He never tired of the process; he was never impatient no matter how trivial the point I was pursuing. He seemed to enjoy revisiting his past.

I also interviewed musicians who worked with Dizzy and knew Dave well, and I reviewed an archival catalogue covering Dave's 50-year relationship with Dizzy that was compiled by Carol Branston, one of Dave's long-time friends.

As I indicated, Dave is really a softy, his salty language and tough exterior notwithstanding. On numerous occasions, when he discussed particularly poignant remembrances, his eyes would tear up, and sometimes he would cry. I must admit, I fought hard to control my emotions when I saw his tears which were sometimes happy ones, and at other times sad, depending on the respective recollections.

One of the truly bewildering aspects of the interviews was that Dave never referred to any records. He did not make any notes or review papers or documents in anticipation of my questions. He did it all from memory. He could recall dates, spellings, and minor details most people would forget within a few days of their occurrence. Not Dave. He remembered everything.

He remembered street addresses and even apartment numbers in buildings he visited decades earlier. For instance, when he told me that in 1948 the American Federation of Musicians (AFM) enforced a recording ban on artists to protest the financial deals offered by record companies, deals it found unacceptable, he explained that the ban was the work of its president, James C. Petrillo. He recalled the AFM president's name, including the middle initial, and this had happened more than 60 years earlier. Actually, I had noticed this aptitude while working for him.

Throughout my relationship with Dave, I was continually impressed by how he engendered admiration and trust from all those who crossed his path, whether the relationships were professional or personal. The reason, I believe, was that he was committed to an uncompromising standard of honesty and integrity. Some may have disagreed with him on issues, but everyone respected him.

Dave also related fascinating stories on how his father was among the first to launch a recycling business by collecting and refining used motor oil, and how he, Dave, helped pioneer the oil spill and hazardous material clean-up industry. Indeed, Dave became one of the world's leading experts in the business.

When President George Herbert Walker Bush asked the U.S. Coast Guard, after the Iraqi dictator, Saddam Hussein, dumped millions of gallons of oil in the Persian Gulf during "Desert Storm" in 1991, who had the best expertise to clean up the oil, he was told "Dave Usher" by U.S. Coast Guard Rear Admiral Joel D. Sipes. The President ordered Dave sent to the Gulf to represent the U.S. as an advisor to the Saudi Arabian government. The assignment almost cost Dave his life when he was caught in quicksand. The headquarters for the operation was located in Dhahran, Saudi Arabia, a coastal city on the Arabian Peninsula. During his first assignment, Dave was on foot inspecting an oil-damaged marsh when he suddenly began to sink. The quicksand was already above his waist when two coworkers managed to grab him under the armpits and pull him out. They literally yanked him out of his waders. When Dave described the incident, he told me, "My waders are still there." One of the men who saved Dave was MPC general manager, Jeff Heard, Dave's godson and nephew of the jazz drummer J.C. Heard.

After the U.S. ended its involvement in the cleanup, Dave was asked to continue work on the project for the International Maritime Organization (IMO) under the auspices of the United Nations. In all, "commuting" back and forth from the U.S. to Saudi Arabia, he spent one year on the Persian Gulf cleanup operation. Specifically, while an IMO representative, he worked for the Saudi's Meteorological and Environmental Protection Agency (MEPA.)

A sensitive problem which had to be faced and solved in assigning Dave to the Gulf was the fact that he was Jewish. Saudi Arabia did not welcome Jews on its soil, frequently prohibiting entry, particularly if they were Israelis. It was an open question whether Dave would be admitted if the Saudis learned that he was Jewish; it was a risk that needed to be addressed. The Coast Guard raised the issue with President Bush, who ignored the implications that a Jew might be barred by the Saudis. The President simply told the Coast Guard, "Have him at hanger No. 6 at National Airport at 0600." (Dave was told of the President's comments to send him to the Gulf and how the President handled the "Jewish issue" by his Coast Guard contacts.)

However, after the U.S. ended its involvement in the cleanup, his religion became an entirely different matter. When Dave traveled on U.S. government aircrafts, he did not have to worry because he did not need to go through customs or have his passport cleared. When he started flying commercial, however, which he would have to do on many occasions, Dave realized he could face serious problems if the Saudis discovered that he was Jewish. IMO officials addressed the problem while Dave was sitting in a Jaguar, the IMO secretary general's car, in London. The solution they proposed was: When filling out the papers required by the Saudis, Dave was instructed to write "n/a" (not applicable) in the space asking him to declare his religion. He followed the advice and told me, "I never had any trouble." Incidentally, while in Saudi Arabia, Dave periodically telephoned Dizzy in the U.S., and each time Dizzy would ask him, "So did you find a good delicatessen yet? Because if I come over, I want to be able to eat some good kosher food."

After we finished the interviews, I began writing, and as chapters were completed, Dave reviewed the drafts, corrected errors, and suggested editorial changes he deemed appropriate.

I could not have had a more rewarding writing experience. I learned about Dizzy Gillespie, about some of the hallowed figures in jazz, and the contributions my friend — and I consider it a privilege to be able to call him my friend — made to this soul-searing music and how, in his other career, he helped protect the environment by developing sophisticated processes and techniques to clean up oil spills and hazardous materials.

In addition, our friendship seemed to grow during the process, and many interviews concluded with the exchange of warm hugs and testimonials on how much we valued the friendship of the other.

It took Dave 20 years to say "yes," and I am delighted he did. I believe we saved some important jazz history (along with a little Detroit history), and I had the opportunity to spend many delightful hours with this engaging man as he told me about his historic relationship and regaled me with countless warm and very moving stories.

"Depression, Blues, Flamenco, Wine, Despair" *

by

Al Young

State of California Poet Laureate Emeritus

Depression, blues, flamenco, wine, despair —
sunk in, they make you cross your heart and die
for hope. Dark times come at you; they don't care.
"So deal with this," they say. And so you buy
the pain and stress, the restlessness — the works:
low back pain, aches and limps, the twitch
of fear your face betrays.

John "Dizzy" Birks
Gillespie's cheeks popped out (fat love an itch
scratched by the trumpet at his goateed lip),
they said: "Take chances, stretch, jump at the sun.
You just can't spend your whole life acting hip.
Be corny sometimes. Have yourself some fun.
You can't be cool forever, so relax."

Diz knew puffed cheeks were anything but chic,
but when you closed your eyes you heard him axe
infinitives, split atoms, hairs. You speak
that tongue — curves, flatlands, all of it. You do.

You understand the hoodoo stab of hurt;
the blues, their messy messages, a few
trashed hopes, some lame goodbyes, her skirt,
your coat, the folded jeans, wet tights. Black night
is falling all around you in the rain.
Dark times, dark times can fix you in the light
of reason, recognition, lasers, pain.

Note From Berl Falbaum

I thought it was important to include this poem about Dizzy Gillespie not only because of its profound insight but because of how I discovered it.

The story begins more than a half century ago when I developed a very special friendship with Al Young over a nine-year period, between 1948-57, when we were classmates in elementary, intermediate and high school. I didn't keep in touch with him after he graduated from the University of Michigan and moved to Berkeley, California where he enjoyed a highly acclaimed career as a novelist, poet, and essayist. He held the position of poet laureate for the State of California between 2005 and 2008.

In 2012, the 1957 alumni of Detroit's Central High School from which he and I graduated, planned a 55-year reunion, and Al flew to Detroit to attend. In the afternoon of the evening celebration, he and I met to talk and relive "our youth" and respective careers. As I described to him in general terms the book I was writing about Dizzy Gillespie and a unique friendship he had enjoyed with a white, Jewish jazz buff, Al responded, "You must be talking about Dave Usher."

It was one of those spooky moments that makes you believe in some "special power" and gives you chills and goose bumps. He knew about Dave and Dizzy, how they launched a record label, Dee Gee Record Company (which Dave describes in Chapter 5) and other elements of their relationship.

Al told me that he had written many poems about celebrities, including one about Dizzy whom he had met several times. As soon as I returned home, I went to Al's website and found the poem.

The issue of using the poem in this book did not require much discussion between Dave and me. Given the circumstances that brought the poem to our attention, we both acknowledged that the gods and fate demanded it be included in this story.

MEETING DIZZY

1

—❖—

We — John Birks "Dizzy" Gillespie and I — were the embodiment of the odd couple. Throughout the years, I often wondered how we developed not only a professional relationship, but a very close personal bond, one that lasted just short of 50 years.

I was born in the North in Detroit; Dizzy was born in the South in Cheraw, South Carolina. I was the youngest of five children; he was the youngest of nine. I had limited musical talent; Dizzy taught himself to play the trombone and trumpet at the age of 10. I grew up in a home that listened exclusively to classical music; Dizzy was exposed to blues and jazz almost from birth, given that his father was a bandleader in Cheraw. I was Jewish; he a believer in the Bahá'í Faith to which he converted when he was about 50. (Dizzy grew up in a Methodist household.) Oh yes, I was white; he was black, or more accurately, colored or Negro as African-Americans were called at the time.

A close relationship between a black and white, whether professional or personal, was still a rarity in the 1940s, even in the North, and yet despite our different histories and the racial sensitivities of the time, we clicked.

If we had one thing in common, it was that we were both the target of discrimination. I was often called a "Jew boy" or "kike" and he a "nigger," if not to our faces, although it happened, then behind our backs. Perhaps

2

the mutual suffering and constant efforts to overcome the hatred of others contributed to our relationship.

There were probably many reasons we bonded; one factor, perhaps the key factor, was music. We both lived and loved it. It was an inseparable part of our lives. It consumed us 24 hours a day; nothing was more important.

As I indicated, my family, as was the case with many Jewish families, was devoted to classical music. Music was played on the radio or a record player in our house almost all the time. My mother loved it, and started taking me to hear the Detroit Symphony Orchestra (DSO) when I was six. I always sat in the same seat on an aisle in the front row. I also attended young people's concerts on school outings.

Even at a young age, less than 10 years old, music left its mark on me. At home — we lived at 2383 Cortland on Detroit's near west side — I would take a serving tray, stand it up, support it with books, pretend it was a podium and "conduct" the music I heard on the radio or record player.

I still remember the conductor, Ossip Salomonowitsch Gabrilowitsch, a world-class musician who was recruited to conduct the DSO by Detroit's power elite. Gabrilowitsch refused to accept the offer to lead the DSO unless the Board of Directors committed itself to building a first-class music hall with the best acoustics that technology allowed at the time. The DSO Board agreed, and Grabrilowitsch's demand led to the construction of Orchestra Hall on Woodward Avenue, Detroit's main thoroughfare, at Parsons, about two miles north of the center of downtown. It was completed in 1919 and the DSO played at the hall until 1939, when financial pressures forced the orchestra to move to the Scottish Rite Cathedral in the Masonic Temple near Cass and Temple. (Gabrilowitsch, who was Mark Twain's son-in-law, conducted the orchestra that played at the ceremonies when my brother, William, graduated from medical school.)

Not only did my mother expose me to music, but my siblings, William, Morris, and Reva, were all musicians. William, a doctor, played the tiple, a 12-string guitar-like instrument, and clarinet; Morris, a pharmacist, played the organ and accordion; and my sister, Reva, played piano, excelled in

3

modern dance, painted, and was an accomplished fencer with the foil. I once saw her beat the Hungarian fencing master Bela de Tuscan.

Reva and I were the black sheep of the family because neither of us was academically inclined. I was a little "blacker" because I lacked patience and did little in school except look out the windows.

This is was not to say I didn't make an attempt. I sang in the Glee Club, and I took piano lessons, but even at an early age, I recognized that I lacked the talent to become a musician. I took piano lessons at the Detroit Music Conservancy, next to the Maccabees Building in midtown Detroit near Wayne State University, with Marian Meckler, the sister-in-law of my brother, William. The fact that I lacked talent became all too evident to me one day while listening to a student who was my tutor's daughter.

I can still see her, Ruthie Meckler, sitting on a piano stool, wearing a blue dress with a pinafore and she played exceedingly well. (She became an accomplished pianist, enjoying an international reputation, and married a famous violinist and conductor, Jaime Laredo.)

I knew instinctively that I would never be able to play at that level. I had what today you might call a "hip" mind, and the fact that I was not in her league, registered with me very quickly and clearly. I already had a competitive nature and I knew I wouldn't be able to compete with her or others with such talents. So why pursue it if I would not be any good at playing the piano? That was the end of my piano lessons.

As to performing, my only stage appearance came when I was the rear end of Ferdinand, the bull, in a production at Roosevelt Elementary School. Yes, I was commended for my performance. I didn't know how to react to compliments that I did well playing the rear end of a bull. Was there an implication in those remarks?

I recognized that the stage was not in my future, but I did have talents at production, promotion and organization. I had what they call in Yiddish *chutzpah* (audacity, brazenness.) I was not afraid to ask for anything even at a young age, and managed to organize several theatrical events in school.

4

I launched one of my first projects with a classmate, David Levine, at Durfee Intermediate School. (Roosevelt, Durfee and the high school I would attend, Central, were all adjacent to each other on Detroit's near west side). We created a very sophisticated puppet show with a large wood and cardboard box that was used to ship gas stoves. We found the box in an alley at Linwood and Elmhurst, hauled it home, and with some amateur carpentry, built a puppet theater with curtains and all the trimmings. We made the puppets from paper mache, wrote the scripts, and my mother sewed the clothing.

At the end of the show, we unfurled the American flag and used a small electric fan to make it wave. For added emphasis, we shook talcum powder in front of the fan, giving the ending of the show a special flavor. We were asked to put on performances for all the homeroom classes in the school. The reaction was excellent, and many in the audiences were so appreciative they gave us money after the shows, money we donated to the Junior Red Cross which had been organized in 1917 to get kids involved in helping the U.S. through World War I, and later World War II.

Incidentally, the puppet project led me to the first and only "criminal" activity in my life. I needed Christmas-type lights for the stage and, having no money, "lifted" them at a dime store. To my chagrin, the owner, Mr. Miller, caught me. I expected severe repercussions, but to my surprise and relief, after a lecture, a mild one at that, Mr. Miller not only let me go, he let me keep the lights. Maybe we should have given Mr. Miller some credit for the staging. Most important, thanks to Mr. Miller's kindness, I avoided creating a police record.

The very positive response to the puppet show reinforced my creative impulses, and boosted my confidence in my production capabilities. A few years later, at Durfee Intermediate, I founded a teenage "night club," Club Jivetown. As I said, I had chutzpah and was not embarrassed or intimidated to ask the city's parks and recreation department if I could "borrow" two trucks, with drivers, of course. We drove to Cass Technical High School where officials agreed to loan me risers, music stands, PA systems, and just about any equipment I needed. The authorities at the parks and recreation department were amazed at my entrepreneurship, and called me a "little pot licker."

I set up the equipment in Durfee's gymnasium and we featured talent from among the students. I also called booking agents, asking them to send musicians, magicians, jugglers and other entertainers.

The club, which operated from 5:30 p.m.-8 p.m. Fridays, received rave reviews, with plaudits coming from school officials, the students, and parents who were grateful for such entertainment to keep their kids off the streets during the country's wartime setting. It was a diversion for everyone.

Detroit, the Arsenal of Democracy, was working 24 hours a day. Our parents, an integral and vital part of this wartime effort, did not have a minute to themselves, and were delighted for any activity — wholesome activity — that kept their children busy.

Meanwhile, during my years in elementary, intermediate and high school, another world opened for me — the world of jazz. I listened to records from my brother Bill's collection which included many that featured jazz. I spent hours listening to jazz and I loved its beat and soul. It grabbed me; it got under my skin. It became an inseparable part of my being.

I listened to Cab Calloway, band leader and singer; Benny Goodman, the genius on the clarinet; the guitarist Charlie Christian; and many others. One day, I played a Calloway record called "Tarzan of Harlem." As the band played, the musicians shouted out, in introducing the solo of a trumpeter, Dizzy Gillespie, "Diz the Wiz, a real horn tooter."

After only a few notes, I was hooked. It was like just reading a page or two in a book and knowing it was written by someone with outstanding talent. I couldn't believe that someone like me, with only a classical music background, could be moved so much by Dizzy's talent. After that, I made a point of listening to jazz, particularly if it featured Dizzy, and bought his records at Al's Record Shop on Broadway near the Broadway-Capitol Theater. I learned about bebop which Dizzy helped develop with such jazz geniuses as Charlie "Bird" Parker, alto saxophone; Kenny Clarke, drums; Thelonious, Monk and Bud Powell, piano; Charlie Christian, guitar, and a few others.

In 1944, when I was 14, I read that Dizzy was scheduled to play at the Paradise Theatre which had moved into the old Orchestra Hall building in 1941, two years after the DSO vacated the site. Dizzy was in the trumpet section and led the Billy Eckstine band. At the time, Eckstine was a huge star as a singer. He was born to a mixed-race couple, William and Nannie Eckstein. I had read that he changed "Eckstein" to "Eckstine" because a club owner told him "Eckstein" was "too Jewish."

The theater, which showed movies along with staging live productions, was named after Paradise Valley — also known as Black Bottom — a black neighborhood in an area bounded roughly by Gratiot, Brush, Hastings, Vernor and Forest. Folklore has it that the area was named after an Asian Paradise tree that was planted along fences.

The Paradise Theatre was principally a black venue — or black-and-tan as it was called at the time — and featured such famous black artists as Billie Holiday, Louis "Satchmo" Armstrong, Pearl Bailey, Duke Ellington, Count Basie and Lena Horne. The Paradise was as dear to the hearts of black Detroiters as the Apollo Theater was to blacks in Harlem. I'd also gone to other black clubs in Paradise Valley, such as El Sino, Club 666 (Three Sixes), Club Plantation, and 606 Horseshoe Lounge.

The theater was not far from the Woodward Show Bar, which my father had opened with several partners, including my brother, Morris, and Ruthie Meckler's father, Ben. It was on the west side of Woodward, next to the defunct Roxy Theater. The bar featured what, at the time, was the longest bar in Michigan. That and the outstanding entertainment attracted Detroiters and men in the service who waited in long lines to get in.

After reading about Dizzy's scheduled appearance at the Paradise, I made plans to see him perform. I bought tickets, borrowed a car from my brother-in-law, Bill Geer, and drove to the theater with a girl who shared my interests in music, particularly jazz. (The authorities eased licensing restrictions in 1944 and permitted 14-year-olds to drive because with so many men in the armed services during the war, families at home needed drivers.)

I was mesmerized by the music. Sure, I enjoyed the DSO and respected the talents of classical musicians. That was not the issue. The issue was that jazz had a special effect on me. When the concert was over, I decided I had to meet "Diz the Wiz" and waited for him inside the stage door entrance. A stage manager challenged me, but when I told him I was determined to meet Dizzy, he relented and let me wait. It wasn't long before Dizzy came along with his wife, Lorraine. I introduced myself, and we had the usual awkward exchanges between a 14-year-old and an adult 11 years older.

I had an idea. Gasoline was scarce because of a truck drivers' strike, and I assumed Dizzy might need a ride. (I was able to get gas for my car because of my father's business connections in the oil industry.) I offered to drive Dizzy and his wife back to their hotel, the Gotham.

The hotel, a nine-story, 200-room hotel, could brag that, over the years, its guests included the likes of heavyweight boxing champion Joe Louis; jazz vocalist Ella Fitzgerald; multi-talented entertainer Sammy Davis, Jr.; future Supreme Court Justice Thurgood Marshall; and many other famous blacks. Unfortunately, the hotel, which also had served as a center for social interaction for blacks, was razed in 1963 when it faced serious financial problems.

Dizzy graciously accepted my offer of a ride. However, there was one problem. The hotel was just one block from the theater on Orchestra Place and John R. Thus, the ride was obviously very short and I didn't have the opportunity to talk with my hero for long. I valued even this brief meeting which, at 14, was a highlight of my life. When we arrived at the hotel, we shook hands and parted.

I don't know what forces led this 14-year-old to begin a relationship with a much older black musician who already was a major celebrity in a war-time environment when the racial divide was almost impregnable. I often asked myself how this happened given that my background was rooted in a white, Jewish, lower middle-income family whose love of music centered on Bach, Mozart, Beethoven, and Ravel.

Despite all our differences, at that encounter by the stage door exit, the seed was planted for a bond that lasted until Dizzy died in January 1993, about a half-century later.

To this day, I am happy that I did not let the stage manager shoo me away. My persistence, some might call it stubbornness, led to an invaluable friendship, one that I reflect on almost daily. It was a gift I cherished throughout my life.

THE USHKATZ (USHER) HISTORY

2

My parents, Charles and Anna Ushkatz (cat's ear) lived in the Ukraine when it was still part of Russia. They had five children: Victor, who died in the Ukraine; William and Morris, who were born in the Ukraine; and Reva and me. Reva and I were born in Detroit; my birthday is December 29, 1929.

(When my oldest brother, William, who became a doctor in Detroit, opened his practice, his patients could not pronounce "Ushkatz" so he changed the name to "Usher." The rest of the family followed his lead.)

My parents were what we would today describe as liberal Conservative Jews which means they went to pray in the synagogue almost exclusively on the two major Jewish holidays — Rosh Hashanah and Yom Kippur. They attended the B'nai David Synagogue on Elmhurst at 14th on Detroit's near west side. The synagogue followed the Orthodox tradition of separating the men and women, and, as a child, I frequently sat with my mother during services. My parents were proud of their heritage and Judaism, and I still have my father's *tallit* (prayer shawl) and prayer books.

In the Ukraine, my father worked as a carpenter, helping to build coaches and wagons. When he recognized that he couldn't make a living, the family decided to immigrate to the United States. My father left first, traveling by ship. He arrived in Winnipeg, Canada in 1908, and worked as a laborer doing odd jobs. After he settled in, he sent for my mother and two brothers.

A few weeks after my mother's arrival, she took in laundry to help pay the family's expenses.

However, the financial situation for the family proved as difficult as in the Ukraine, so my parents decided to move once more. Again, my father left first, and got a job feeding cattle on a train heading for slaughter in Chicago. From Chicago, he "hoboed" on a train to Detroit. He chose Detroit because he thought he could use his carpentry skills in the auto industry since most car parts in those days were made of wood.

In Detroit, he was hired at Ford Motor Co.'s Rouge Plant which, ironically, was near where I would headquarter my environmental services company, Marine Pollution Control (MPC), many years later. He discovered his carpentry skills were of no value. My father was assigned to work as a stevedore on the docks, unloading ships that carried ore, soy bean, coal and other products. After he once again felt secure, he sent for my mother and two brothers.

At Ford, my father received a flat weekly salary, but he learned that the now-defunct Packard Motor Car Co. on East Grand Boulevard paid according to piece work. Since he was a hard worker, he knew he could make more money at Packard.

He wanted to quit but faced one problem. If he resigned, he would have to wait to get paid and return to the plant for his money. My father wanted to avoid the hassle of going back for his pay. The travel alone from our house on Cortland and LaSalle to the Ford plant was extremely time-consuming and inconvenient. If he were fired, he would be paid on his way out the door. He knew what he had to do. He walked onto a ship he was unloading, went to the officers' mess hall, which was a very big "no-no," sat down in an officer's chair and put his feet up on a table covered by a tablecloth. It wasn't too long before he was discovered and summarily fired. He got his money immediately and left.

He was hired at Packard and worked on the assembly line hanging car doors. Now he was paid for each door he hung, and he worked as fast as possible. The assembly line had two sides, and across from my father worked a man named Cherry. Cherry, who became a family friend, couldn't keep up with the pace my father set and worried that he might be fired. So my father made him a proposal: After he finished his own work, he would run to Cherry's side and help him catch up. My father offered the deal on one condition: Cherry would have to pay him half for each door my father hung for him.

Cherry accepted, paid my father the 50 percent, and was grateful that he didn't lose his job. The vision of my father running from side to side always reminded me of the scene with the famous silent movie comic, Charlie Chaplin, in which he worked on an assembly line. As only Chaplin could, given his genius, he captured the nuances of that kind of repetitive work.

The major point of the story to me was that my father, a carpenter with no business background, suddenly became a businessman. He saw an opportunity and made it work. Cherry recognized that my father's offer was fair, and he and my father remained friends for a long time. I always thought that my father's effort to help Cherry showed my father's *Yiddishkeit* (Jewish humanity) in wanting to assist his friend, and indicated he had an acumen for business.

During this period, a cousin, Leon Komisaruk, lived with my parents on Cortland. A graduate of Ohio State University, he was a bright guy with a degree in chemical engineering. He became a petroleum engineer. He had dedicated himself to helping other members of the family get out of Russia. He traveled back and forth continually, bribing Russian border guards, and he managed to help many relatives flee the country.

Periodically, Komisaruk would ask my father to invest in business proposals that he assured my father would make him a rich man. One involved producing a new candy, and in another venture, they would manufacture perfume. Needless to say, these financial endeavors failed. Things got so bad that my father, for a while, wouldn't even talk to Komisaruk.

Then came the depression years and my father lost his job. Komisaruk approached him again and, after numerous attempts, Komisaruk finally convinced my father to listen. He told him to buy a flat-bed truck and pick up used motor oil from gas stations in a 100-gallon wooden barrel.

My father, under Komisaruk's plan, would then deliver the oil to Komisaruk, who would "re-refine" the oil before selling it. The re-refined oil was actually of a better quality than the original product and also cheaper. With his back against the wall, my father agreed.

In 1929-30, Komisaruk and two partners formed the Keystone Oil Refining Co. on Schaefer at Fort Street, and my father founded Usher Waste Oil Service on Detroit's near west side. I believe their efforts may have been the first recycling program in the oil business.

Komisaruk's partners were:

William Fisher, father of Max M. Fisher, who would become an oil and real estate magnate, world diplomat and philanthropist, and Nathan Epstein, a businessman. Max Fisher worked for Keystone for $15 a week for a brief period before founding his own company which became the largest gas station chain in the Midwest. He sold it to Aurora Oil, which he chaired for 27 years, before it merged with Speedway and the Ohio Oil Co. to become Marathon Oil.

Ironically, Max Fisher's history also overlaps in my music world. After the Paradise Theatre was forced to close in 1951, the building stood vacant for about 20 years. In 1970, plans were begun to renovate the structure, but it took 20 years before work was completed. It became the home again for the DSO in 1989. In 2002-03, it was renovated and expanded significantly under a $60 million project spearheaded by Max Fisher. The complex is called the Max M. Fisher Music Center, with Detroiters calling it, affectionately, "The Max."

Eugene Epstein, the son of Nathan Epstein, in years to come, would form Vesco Oil Corp. with two partners, Aaron Silverman and Harry Victor. Eugene Epstein, Silverman and Victor took the first letter of their last names and added "co" to create "Vesco." Eugene Epstein would head Vesco Oil as his sons, Richard and Donald, would in later years.

It is fascinating to reflect that two of Komisaruk's partners, who had business relationships with my father's company, went on to create huge enterprises. With the success of Keystone, Komisaruk paid my father back for all the

14

failures. It was so successful that the oil companies, afraid of being undercut by the cheaper prices of the re-refined oil, tried to have legislation passed in Congress that would levy a special tax on recycled oil.

My brother, Morris, became a partner in Usher Waste Oil Service, owning 50 percent of the business. A licensed pharmacist, he opted out of practicing his profession because he didn't want to stand on his feet 10-12 hours a day behind a counter. After my father died in 1960, he bequeathed his 50 percent to Reva and me. Morris, after he passed away in 1984, left his half to his wife, Sophie, who sold it to her son, Michael. Michael bought out Reva's and my share and continued to operate the company. Reva died in 2005.

As my parents worked toward financial security, they constantly worried about me. To put it mildly, I was a lousy student. School simply bored me, and teachers could not keep me from staring out the windows. With two brothers who were academic achievers — one a doctor and the other a pharmacist — my parents couldn't understand how they had failed with me or what to do about it.

In addition to the secular public schools, I also attended the *Arbeter Ring* (Yiddish for Workmen's Circle) for my religious training. The *Arbeter Ring*, which my father joined, was organized in 1900 by immigrants from Eastern Europe, many of them with Socialist tendencies. It was a labor fraternal order dedicated to social justice, offering a wide variety of activities. Its educational focus, however, was very progressive and emphasized Jewish culture and history rather than religious ritual and tradition. Also, while other Jewish schools taught in Hebrew, the language at the *Arbeter Ring* was Yiddish.

Given the secular orientation of the *Arbeter Ring*, I never had a bar mitzvah, the religious service that ushers a boy into adulthood when he turns 13. But I did have a bar mitzvah under very unique circumstances many years later — in 2012 — when I was 82 and flying at some 31,000 feet on a Delta Airlines flight from New York to London.

I was prepared for a routine flight when I boarded the plane in New York, and sat next to an Orthodox Jew. The man, who was in early 20s, turned

15

out to be a Sephardic rabbi from France who spoke English haltingly. So, I asked him if he spoke Yiddish. The rabbi's eyes lit up and, for the next few hours, we chatted about a variety of subjects.

At one point, I explained that as a boy, I attended the *Arbeter Ring* in Detroit for my religious training. As a result, while fluent in Yiddish, which I spoke at school and at home with my parents, I told the rabbi that I had never had a bar mitzvah. Without hesitating, the rabbi replied: "Well, you're going to have one now." When the rabbi said "now," he meant "now."

From a package stowed in the overhead bin, the rabbi brought out a *tallit* (prayer shawl), *tefillin* (cube-shaped black leather boxes, containing scriptural passes which are attached to the head and arm and worn during morning prayers), and a prayer book. He put the *tallit* over my shoulders, the *tefillin* on my arm and forehead, and after learning that I did not speak, read, write or understand Hebrew, asked me to simply repeat the prayers he would recite.

With the passengers watching in puzzlement, the rabbi conducted a 10-minute service, and when he concluded he told me: "Now you had a bar mitzvah."

I was not embarrassed in having this bar mitzvah on the plane. I was elated. Frankly, it was a highlight in my life for this to happen when I was 82 years old and under these somewhat strange circumstances.

When the plane landed, the crew, standing by the cockpit, congratulated me. They were all smiles. I think it is safe to say they had never seen this on their plane before. No one threw candy at me as they do at the end of the more traditional service in a synagogue. But a flight attendant told me while she was not Jewish, her husband was. Then, instead of throwing candy, she served me a kosher meal.*

Along with my "official" studies, I immersed myself in jazz — totally. I had no technical skills in music; I couldn't read sheet music. Whatever I had learned during my piano lessons, I had already forgotten. But despite these

---

*A feature story on my bar mitzvah was published in the *Detroit Jewish News* in August 2013.

musical deficiencies, from the beginning, I could differentiate between good jazz and bad, pros from amateurs.

In addition to listening to my brother Bill's jazz collection in Grosse Pointe, Michigan, an affluent Detroit suburb, another major jazz influence on me was a kid, Moe Lyons, a friend of the family. He lived in Edmonton, Alberta, Canada, and when I visited my uncle, Mayer Comisarow, in Edmonton, Moe would take me to places that sold records that were worn because they'd been used in jukeboxes. We didn't care. Given the wear and tear on the records, they were extremely cheap. We bought them (I still own some) and listened endlessly even though the quality was poor.

In Detroit, I was a regular customer at Al's Record Shop on Broadway in downtown. I also read magazines dedicated to jazz such as *Metronome*, which went out of business in 1961, and *DownBeat*, which was still publishing in 2013 when I recorded these remembrances.

My parents thought I was *meshugeh* (crazy.) All their son did and wanted to do was listen to jazz. What's with this jazz, schmazz? What's with this kid? *Oy*, did they worry. No, he didn't have "criminal" tendencies; he didn't get involved with police authorities. That was the good news. The bad news was that he wouldn't study, he received low grades, and he didn't seem to care. And they weren't wrong in their assessments; I simply didn't have any interest in studying.

When I was in the 10th grade at Central, my sister-in-law, Bella Usher, gave my parents the names of private schools which were dedicated to helping "problem" children, children that needed discipline. My parents showed me the names, telling me I would have to attend one of the schools, but that I could select which one. The decision was an easy one for me. I chose the Admiral Farragut Academy on the banks of the Toms River in Pine Beach, New Jersey because it focused on ships and the seas — naval studies — which, next to jazz, were among my primary interests.

The academy was named after David Glasgow Farragut, a Civil War naval hero who is credited with the famous line: "Damn the torpedoes. Full speed ahead!" He allegedly shouted it during the 1864 Battle of Mobile Bay in

Alabama where the Mobile and Tensaw Rivers meet and flow into the Gulf of Mexico. (He was referring to tethered mines and not, of course, torpedoes as we know them.) Those who graduated from Farragut usually enrolled in a military academy for their higher education studies.

As a young boy, I had been a member of a private organization called the Young Seamen of America (YSA) which was located near the Detroit River on property that, years later, would become Detroit's Civic Center. We wore Navy-like uniforms and our berets had "YSA" embroidered on them. When asked what the letters stood for, we generally gave one of two answers: "You Shouldn't Ask" or "the Yugoslavian Submarine Academy." In the YSA, I learned the nomenclature of the sea, how to tie knots, and many other skills related to life on the sea.

At the same time, when the family vacationed in Charlevoix, in the northern part of Michigan's Lower Peninsula, I would visit a three-man U.S. Coast Guard rescue station. A petty officer — Officer McDonald — always invited me in, and it was not long before I was sweeping floors, cleaning boats and doing other minor chores. At times, he even permitted me to answer the radio transmissions, and callers must have been mystified to hear "Charlevoix Light Boat Station" coming from the voice of a 13-year-old. I was elated; I was in seventh heaven.

In 1950, I joined the U.S. Coast Guard Organized Reserve Unit Training, Port Security (ORUTPS), and I was a member for about two years. Basically, the unit's responsibility was to assure the security of ports in the U.S.

Despite Admiral Farragut's courageous command, I did not charge full speed ahead at the school. I performed as badly at Farragut as I had in Detroit schools. I was always on the list of students receiving demerits, called "sticks" at Farragut. Nor was I a very good marksman. I was called "Grim Death" because the only way I had a chance of hitting a bull's-eye would be on a lucky ricochet. After about a year, I dropped out and returned to Detroit.

I gave school one more shot. I enrolled in Detroit's Cooley High School at Hubbell and Chalfonte on the city's northwest side. To enroll, I used a friend's address because I didn't live in the school's district. The outcome was the same. I dropped out again and that was my final and futile attempt to earn a high school diploma.

I went to work for my father, primarily as a truck driver, delivering oil to my cousin's oil re-refinery company. By that time, my father had developed three lines of business: Collecting used motor oil to be re-refined by Komisaruk; selling oil to be applied to gravel roads to control dust; and picking up salvage or waste oil delivered by tankers into a huge pit, oil that, for a variety of reasons, could not be used in the manufacture of steel. I frequently picked up tanker oil that was skimmed off the top that was useable. Actually, they gave us that oil at no cost just to get rid of it. We would refine it and sell it back to them as useable oil.

I learned about oil, its various uses, and the business opportunities it offered. While my father was what I called a "liquid junkman," my experiences, which proved invaluable in my life, led me to become an "environmentalist," long before that term became part of our political culture and the public dialogue.

My next job, which I got with the help of my father, was with an air conditioner manufacturer, American Thermal Industries (ATI) on Illinois, two blocks east of Woodward and about five miles north of downtown Detroit. My father was a minority shareholder in the company and used his "connections" with the majority investors to have management hire me.

I did a variety of odd jobs that didn't require special skills. Here I learned important lessons in labor relations. The atmosphere was tense because the supervisor was harassing one man who was not "too quick" but he was a decent man. The rest of us decided to protest and while we didn't have a union, we filed grievances. When management turned a deaf ear, we organized a sit-down. I was part of a protest against a company in which my father was an owner. In any case, we made our point, and the company implemented policies that protected not only the abused employee but also the rest of us.

19

Interestingly, a major investor in ATI was Morris Schaver, whose wife, Emma, was an opera singer. She performed around the world, and starred with the DSO. She also was a staunch supporter of Israel and one of Detroit's most prominent philanthropists.

For a few months, I also worked for a direct mail company owned by Dave Victor, a distant relative. I earned 45 cents an hour and, among other skills, learned to set type because the company's offices were housed in the Aronson Printing Company on Lafayette, a few miles west of downtown Detroit. That's where I printed the materials for the first record label I would launch about two years later.

EMANON: TURNING INTO A JAZZ PRODUCER

3

—☛—

All was not lost while I was at the Farragut Academy. Why? Because it was during my "studies" at Farragut that I had the opportunity to cement my friendship with Dizzy Gillespie. When we had liberty on weekends, I made my way to New York City. I researched where Dizzy was playing and met him at the clubs. My first meeting with him in New York was at the Spotlite on 52nd Street where several jazz clubs were located in the 1940s. (Dizzy and his big band recorded an album, "Showtime at the Spotlite, 52nd Street, New York City, June 1946.") He remembered our encounter at the Paradise Theatre, and embraced me. I would see him as often as I could and he would welcome me every time and, on occasion, invite me to his apartment at 116th Street and 7th Avenue in Harlem.

I can't explain why an internationally famous black jazz musician was drawn to a white teenager. Perhaps he was intrigued by a white Jewish kid who had an uncompromising passion for jazz. I don't know what he saw, but I was grateful that when I reached out to him, he didn't turn or push me away. Instead, he and I developed "into people." We became the two Ds — Dizzy and Dave.

Dizzy also knew that I had produced a concert in Detroit after our black housekeeper, recognizing my interest in jazz, introduced me to a Detroit bass player, Burrell Dudley, who had an orchestra. His music was the kind of genre I liked, and we became soul mates. When his orchestra had difficulties finding venues for rehearsals, I convinced the authorities at Durfee Intermediate School to let the musicians use the school's music room.

For my proposed concert, I recruited members of Dudley's orchestra and other Detroit jazz musicians. My father and a close friend of the family, James "Jimmy" Montante, a lawyer, who was appointed to a judgeship by Michigan Governor John Swainson and served for almost 20 years on the Wayne County Circuit Court bench, worried about how I would pay the musicians. They kept a close eye on me because they thought I was going down a very dangerous road.

The musicians probably agreed to a business deal with a producer only 15 years old because of the relationship I had developed with Dudley. He vouched for me, despite my age. I'm not sure why they joined my effort. They didn't ask for any money up front because, I believe, they were just delighted to have a place to play and showcase their talents. Whatever the reasons for their participation, the concert, "Modern American Music," at the Maccabees Building in March 1945, was hailed by the musicians and, most importantly, by the audience. I preened.

Now, I took a major step into the record business. As I indicated, I always had a little bit of *chutzpah,* so believing I had sufficient skills to produce my first commercial record, in 1948, when I was 18, I launched the Emanon ("no name" spelled backwards) Record Co. Emanon, which was my first trademark, was the name of a record Dizzy produced in 1945.* He never told me why he chose the name, but knowing Dizzy, I am confident he had a reason for using Emanon. I thought the timing was good for me because the American Federation of Musicians (AFM), led by its president, James C. Petrillo, banned musicians from making any records in the U.S. in protest of the unfair terms offered by record companies. The boycott was called the "Petrillo Ban."

---

*In my research for this book, I discovered another Emanon label was created in Tulsa, Oklahoma in 1999. It had no connection with my label or Dizzy's record.

(Incidentally, the AFM Local No. 5 in Detroit and Local No. 802 in New York were both integrated. In Los Angeles, the union had two locals, one for blacks and one for whites.)

Dizzy and his band were headed to Europe for a tour, and using my *Yiddishe kop* (Jewish head), I concocted an elaborate, complex and devious plan to record him overseas along with some other musicians. After all, the ban did not cover Europe. Emanon records would have a sketch of the Eiffel Tower on its label because we would be recording in Parisian studios. When I discussed the plan with Dizzy, he just laughed.

In anticipation of making the record, I spent a lot of time at the United Sound Systems Recording Studios, a two-family house on Second and Antoinette in a neighborhood that later would be called the New Center Area. United Sound Systems was a major Detroit recording studio, opening its doors in 1933. It was owned by Jimmy Siracuse, and his son, Joe, was the studio engineer. That's where I met Berry Gordy, who was about 11 years away from creating the legendary Motown Records label.

I couldn't get Dizzy involved because he was under contract with RCA-Victor, a subsidiary of the Radio Corporation of America, created when it acquired the Victor Talking Machine Co. in 1929. Instead, I worked with his drummer, Kenny Clarke. I asked for help from Clarke because I needed large crates for my metal acetate master discs, the kind of crates drummers used to carry their instruments. Clarke was supportive because he knew of my relationship with Dizzy. True, while there were other whites in the business, few had established the mutual trust with black artists that Dizzy and I enjoyed. Clarke and I became close friends and I highlighted on the record's label that the compositions featured "Kenny Clarke's All Stars." The pieces were entitled "Out of Nowhere," "Confirmation," "Too Much Horn," and "Tall Boy, Third Row." The last piece was named for Bob Murphy, a Detroit radio disc jockey. He was very tall, and always had to sit in the third row with shorter people in front of him.

Clarke's job was to pack master discs that I would use to make the recordings in his crates. In Paris, Clarke had the help of a famous jazz writer, Charles Delaunay, who had all the necessary contacts. Delaunay was a fervent jazz enthusiast, founder of *Le Jazz Hot*, a highly respected jazz magazine, and in 1948 he created his own record label called Disques Vogue.

The deal we struck was that the material was mine, but Delaunay would have the rights to the music in France. The records were 78s (recorded at 78 rpms — revolutions per minute), as most records were at the time. Other speeds, 33 1/3 and 45, produced a higher quality, but were not instituted until about four years later. The quality of the 33s and 45s was actually much better than even the four-track and eight-track cartridges or CDs produced in later years.

The American musicians on the records were: Clarke, drums; John Brown, alto sax; Cecil Payne, baritone sax; Benny Bailey, trumpet; Al McKibbon and Percy Heath, bass; Howard McGhee, trumpet; John Lewis, piano; and John Collins, guitar. Two others, Jacques Diéval, piano, and Michel de Villers, alto and baritone sax, were French. I made two records and Dizzy is featured on one of them. On the label, I identified him as Saint John so he wouldn't be accused of violating his contractual obligations with RCA-Victor. In the past, on other records Dizzy had used the pseudonym B. Bopstein.

Musicians such as the sensational clarinetist, Benny Goodman, occasionally adopted pseudonyms to get around their contracts. Goodman called himself Shoeless Joe Jackson after the baseball player who, in 1919 as a member of the Chicago White Sox, was accused with other players of conspiring to fix the World Series that year.

Charlie "Yardbird" Parker (later referred to as just "Bird") called himself "Charlie Chan," the name of the fictional Chinese detective, and Chan was also his wife's name. The pseudonym appears on the album, "Jazz at Massey Hall" which was a recording of the famous concert sponsored by the Toronto New Jazz Society in 1953 at Massey Hall in Toronto. The concert featured "The Quintet" and it included Parker, sax; Dizzy, trumpet; Bud Powell, piano; Charles Mingus, bass; and Max Roach, drums.

Years later, the famous vocalist Tony Bennett, asked us to record his piano accompanist, Ralph Sharon, and we agreed. Bennett watched the session in the studio. Then he heard a song he did not know, but loved its tempo. So Bennett joined in and scatted. But on the album, I made no mention

25

of Bennett, not even in the liner notes on the back of the record cover. We entitled the record, "2:38 a.m.: Ralph Sharon & Friend." Since jazz enthusiasts knew that Sharon was Bennett's piano player, they concluded it was Bennett scatting and, of course, they also recognized Bennett's voice. We used "2:38 a.m." in the title because that's when the recording session began.

The companies holding contracts with celebrity artists probably saw through the scheme, but made a decision, for whatever reasons, not to sue. I believe they adopted a hands-off policy because if the records sold, it would give indirect publicity to the artists they had under contract. The record companies' only interest was to assure that the musicians didn't use their real names in violation of contractual agreements. As far as I know, none of the musicians who adopted pseudonyms ended up in court.

When Clarke came home, I pressed about 2,000 records and hit the streets. I was the producer of the record, and distributor as well. In Detroit, Chicago, and New York, I went to radio stations and met with DJs to promote the record. I visited music stores asking them to carry the record. I went to neighborhoods where the brothers and sisters lived, walking up and down the streets with two boxes of records. When I mentioned Dizzy, there was no resistance; I was welcomed. In Detroit, the record was carried by the distributor, Cadet, located next to the Paradise Theatre where I had met Dizzy a few years earlier.

Actually, it wasn't difficult to convince managers of music stores. Dizzy was big. He was a world celebrity, and when I told them that the musicians were members of Dizzy's orchestra, they didn't hesitate to get on board. Dizzy was so famous that a caricature of his face became a symbol for jazz music at the time. It consisted of an outline of a man's head which sported a goatee and a beret. That was Dizzy.

By chance, in one store in Chicago, I met a record salesman, and when he heard that I was a "one-man outfit," he invited me to meet his boss, Monroe B. "Monty" Passis who was running a jazz record distributing company called Chord Distributors. We made a deal; I signed a contract. Now I, had two distributors, Cadet and Chord.

In Detroit, I turned my entire attention to jazz, producing records at an amateur level, working to understand how recordings were manufactured and distributed, and learning as much about the world of jazz as I could. I did all this while working for my father at Usher Waste Oil Service.

When word spread about the Emanon record in the world of jazz, everyone knew that Dizzy had to be involved. The company, by my conservative standards at the time, did very well, and I was pleased that my scheme had worked.

Most important, it was another step in bringing Dizzy and me closer together.

DIZZY TRADEMARKS

4

Dizzy had five special "trademarks" that helped make him so recognizable: His nickname, his "bent" trumpet, his cheeks which would blow up like huge balloons when he played, a rhythm cane he invented and, as I mentioned in the previous chapter, the outline of the head of a jazz musician wearing a beret and goatee.

His nickname: He was already known as "Dizzy" when I met him at the Paradise Theatre in 1944. Through the years, Dizzy told me several times how he acquired the nickname, and the circumstances are recounted in his 1980 autobiography, *To Be, or Not...To Bop: Dizzy Gillespie,* which he wrote with Al Fraser.

As Dizzy tells it in the book, around 1935 he was auditioning with Frankie Fairfax's band, one of the best black bands at the time. The sheet music he was given had pencil marks on them, and they confused him. He had trouble reading the music, didn't play well, and failed the audition. Dizzy quotes Bill Doggett, jazz pianist and a member of the Fairfax band, as saying, "That little dizzy cat's from the South, carries his horn around in a paper bag. You know he can't read." The nickname didn't stick at the time. About a year later, after Dizzy became a member of the Fairfax band, another trumpeter, Palmer "Fats" Davis, reflecting on Dizzy's non-stop antics, used the adjective "dizzy" continually, stating, "Man, this cat is a dizzy cat." Dizzy was branded and never again called by his given name.

Regarding Dizzy's failed audition, Donald L. Maggin, in his book, *The Life and Times of John Birks Gillespie*, maintains that the notes Dizzy had to use at the first audition were purposely written in a "squiggly, unorthodox style" as part of a conspiracy to have Dizzy fail the audition. A trumpeter, Joe Facio, along with Doggett, gave Dizzy the sheet music with the confusing notations because Facio, knowing of Dizzy's talent, worried that if Dizzy got the job, he — Facio — would lose some of his solos.

The trumpet: Dizzy was playing at Snookie's on 45th Street in New York on January 6, 1953, the birthday of his wife, Lorraine. Dizzy met Lorraine in 1937 when she was in a chorus line at the Apollo Theater in Harlem. They married in 1940, and had been married for 53 years when Dizzy died of pancreatic cancer in 1993. Lorraine died at 84 in 2004.

Dizzy had invited many jazz artists and friends to the club to help celebrate. During the evening, he left his trumpet on a stand while he was being interviewed. Members of a dance/comedy act, Stump 'n Stumpy, were clowning around on stage when someone fell and knocked the trumpet off its stand, bending the bell upward.

Despite being angry at the damage to his trumpet, Dizzy continued to play and discovered that the trumpet produced a sound he liked. The bent bell brought the sound "quicker" to his ears, he said, and with the bell turned up, it was easier to read sheet music on a stand because he didn't have to tip the trumpet down as much as he did with a straight bell.

When he told me about the benefits of an angled bell, I suggested he ask the Martin Band Instrument Company in Elkhart, Indiana to make a trumpet for him with the bell angled upward. He contacted the company which had a special committee, the Martin Committee, composed of the best trumpeter designers at the time. Martin, which produced trumpets for other renowned jazz musicians, agreed to Dizzy's strange request and manufactured the trumpet with a 45-degree angle.

I know that some Gillespie biographers were suspicious of the story Dizzy told about the trumpet being bent when someone fell on it. They have written that, during his travels, Dizzy had seen others use an angled bell, tried the trumpet, liked it and had one manufactured for himself. I have no reason to doubt Dizzy's story.

Cheeks: When Dizzy played, his cheeks ballooned out making him look, he said, "like a frog." Conventional wisdom had it that Dizzy never had proper instructions on how to keep his cheeks taut and thus, his cheeks blew out, continually expanding over the years.

Dizzy wasn't sure why his cheeks bulged out, as he says in his autobiography. He writes that Dr. Richard J. Compton, of NASA, wanted to X-ray Dizzy's cheeks to determine the reason for the condition that Compton called "Gilliespie's Pouches." Dizzy didn't keep his appointment with Compton, and in a footnote in his book, he said that, "I prefer to let it (the bulging of the cheeks) remain a mystery."

During a 1985 trip to Cuba, reflecting on his cheeks, Dizzy said, "I don't know what happened to my face. My face just went that way and that's it. I just sort of worry about it a little bit...when I get around 80 or something

Dizzy blowing his horn, cheeks ballooning.

like that, when I get 80, will my jaws withstand the pressure?" He was 67 at the time; sadly, Dizzy died at 75.

Another time, he told ABC news anchor, Peter Jennings, who was doing a short profile on Dizzy when he turned 75: "It's like someone blowing into a balloon." Then Dizzy added, "But it doesn't hurt."

There may be some truth to the theory that he didn't receive proper tutoring as a youngster when he first started playing. However, the ballooning of his cheeks may also have been caused by a medical condition that involves weakness of the *orbicularis oris* (lip) muscle which affects brass players, particularly trumpet and French horn players.

Dizzy told me that he had been examined by doctors on the East Coast who found some weakness in the muscle around his lips as well as the buccinators (muscles at the side of the mouth.)

The trumpet legend Louis "Satchmo" Armstrong actually tore a lip muscle, and had to quit playing for a year in 1935. His condition was labeled "Satchmo's Syndrome" by the medical community.

Addressing Dizzy's condition, Dr. Bernard L. Kaye, a plastic surgeon and a musician himself who died in 2008, had written: "When the Diz blows, his cheeks puff out like a blowfish. One can justifiably postulate attenuation and stretching of the buccinators fibers, so severe that only the physical tensile strength of his cheek skin contains the pressure he needs to vibrate his lips. In his (Dizzy's) case, it is obvious that his rather odd blowing technique is more than adequate to produce his delightful music."

Rhythm cane: Much has been written in books and articles about Dizzy's cheeks, trumpet and nickname, yet little, if anything, has been said about his rhythm cane. Yes, his rhythm cane, which was not only a Gillespie trademark, but also symbolic of Dizzy's musical creativity.

The rhythm cane was Dizzy's invention, consisting of a stick about three feet long and an inch square. Dizzy collected bottle caps of different sizes and would drive a nail through about five caps. Then he would hammer the nail into the stick. Each side of the stick had about 12 nails with the caps, and they were arranged very carefully so that Dizzy could make use of the distinct tones produced by different caps. Dizzy was very exact about the process. When on stage, he would stomp the stick or shake it, and it helped him keep a beat on stage.

The rhythm cane had a specific musical purpose, and to me it was another example of Dizzy's genius, his talent to innovate, and his courage to be unorthodox. The rhythm cane itself was a minor detail in Dizzy's music, of course, but it was reflective of a mind that had no boundaries, one that was prepared to venture into the unknown to help create the best jazz music possible.

Caricature. The other trademark was the outline drawing of a jazz musician (Dizzy) wearing a beret and a goatee. It appeared on posters everywhere — in jazz clubs, music magazines, concert halls — and served as a logo for him at the time. It penetrated the public's consciousness, and helped make him recognizable to jazz enthusiasts.

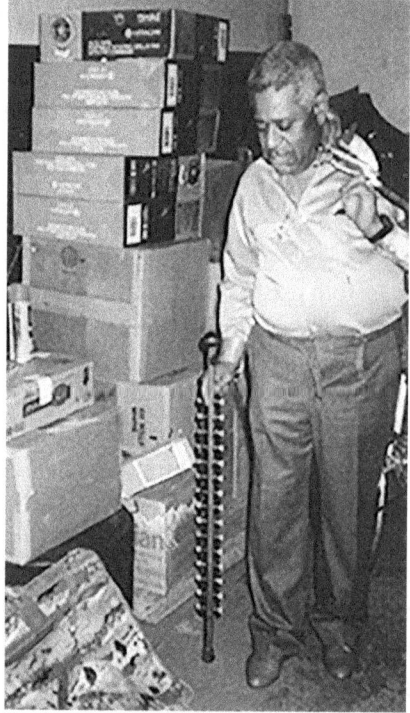

Dizzy with his rhythm cane.

DEE GEE

5

—●—

I had worked on the Emanon label for about two years when Dizzy approached me in 1951, stating he was very unhappy at Capitol Records. He had switched to Capitol from RCA-Victor, not because he was particularly dissatisfied but because he saw what he considered additional opportunities at Capitol. At the time, Capitol was a growing company on the West Coast, and it represented such artists as the all-time celebrated vocalist Frank Sinatra and songwriter Johnny Mercer.

It wasn't working for Dizzy. He said Capitol asked him to play music he considered too commercial, music he didn't really like. He wanted to "educate" the public on the music he had developed — bebop — with Parker. Parker received more credit than Dizzy for the innovation of bebop because he attracted more than his share of media attention. He was a character and his personal problems, which included heavy use of drugs and alcohol, made him the subject of extensive media coverage. But Dizzy had as much a hand in the creation of bebop as Parker, if not more. Other musicians, some of Dizzy's closest friends, also contributed to bebop's development.

Dizzy and Parker were close friends, neither one jealous of the other. They were, in my view, equal as performers. As I said, Dizzy was not critical of the fact that Parker received more than his share of publicity for being a, if not the, creator of bebop. I think Dizzy let it go, hoping that it would counter-balance the negative press Parker received on his alcohol and drug problems. In the end, for all his boisterous antics, Dizzy was a very sensitive guy.

At Capitol, the proverbial straw that broke the back for Dizzy was when Capitol requested, or demanded may be a more accurate word, he record "You Stole My Wife, You Horse Thief." I don't know who wrote it but that was it for Dizzy. The piece had nothing to do with his musical personality, or his skills. He recorded the piece because he was under contract, but he couldn't take it anymore. He was very depressed. He said he couldn't work for a company that produced such material.

As he complained about Capitol, Dizzy suggested that we start our own label. I was flattered, of course. I was only 21 years old, and here was a very famous musician asking me to be his partner and produce his music.

This was at a time when black musicians were exploited by many white agents, distributors, and executives running record companies. The black jazz community had a deep mistrust, and rightly so, of those who produced and sold their music. They knew they were being used, but given the racial divide of the times, and the fact that color barriers were impenetrable, if black artists wanted their music recorded and distributed, they had to put their futures into the hands of many who would not give them a fair shake. They had no choice.

Frank Kofsky, a jazz historian, wrote in his book, *Black Music, White Business: Illuminating the History and Political Economy of Jazz*:

"…Jazz musicians are perennially in the position of having to sell their creativity in a buyers' market, a state of affairs that, as they and the white executives who profit from their talents both are aware, drastically reduces their power to bargain for the kind of treatment that benefits a serious musical artist."

Kofsky added, "In this relative powerless vis-à-vis the white executive opens the way to the qualitatively heightened exploitation of the jazz musician, the disdain with which the former [white] regards the latter [black] makes such exploitation a virtual certainty."

(Kofsky published his book in 1998, and I noticed he wrote in the present tense, meaning he believed that black jazz musicians were still being exploited.)

I was more than delighted that I had Dizzy's trust, particularly in this era of bitter racial tensions, and his proposal told me he knew he had mine. I concluded that he felt comfortable with me, despite my young age and lack of experience.

The issues of race, inexperience, organizational shortcomings, and other key issues, frankly, were never discussed. I had learned the basics of the business and had the knowledge needed to produce records. We had the kind of confidence in each other that permitted this partnership to become a reality. So, after he made the suggestion, we said, "Yeah, let's get together, brother," and just went ahead.

Our discussions led to the creation of the Dee Gee Record Company. Dizzy's wife created the logo. "Dee" was set vertically and "Gee" at the bottom, horizontally forming a right angle. I was responsible for running the company while Dizzy supplied the talent. Under our agreement, we would share the profits 50-50, although we never enjoyed profits to share. If there ever was a labor of love, this was it.

Finances were a major problem. Dizzy didn't have any money to invest. I "plowed" in about $2,000, money I had saved working as a truck driver for Usher Waste Oil. I was earning about $175 a week driving a truck and marketing my father's services. I had about $100 to invest weekly into Dee Gee. To say we were undercapitalized is, obviously, an understatement. We, which means I, paid the musicians a maximum of $40.25 for three hours, or for recording four sides on 78 records. The 78s sold for less than one dollar a piece — about 89 cents — and after the distributors and retailers took their shares, Dee Gee received between 42-45 cents per record. Dee Gee's "world" headquarters were in the basement at 4015 Leslie on Detroit's west side, the home my parents had moved into after leaving their house on Cortland.

I did have some help from friends: Ray Glassman, a classmate years earlier; Marvin Jacobs, who was a collector of Dixieland music, worked for a music distributor and had been in the same Boy Scout troop with me; and Eddie Bierman, also a former classmate. When their time permitted, they assisted with a variety of functions. For artwork, I turned to Art Schurgin, who produced streamers I hung in record stores to promote Dee Gee's records. Schurgin was a big-time promoter and publicity man in Detroit and very influential. He even helped bring The Beatles to the U.S. after they hit the big time in the early 1960s.

The creation of the label caused quite a buzz in the jazz world. The music community was talking about a *schvartze* (black) and a *yid* (Jew) getting together. Magazines such as *Billboard* and *Cashbox*, along with several others, published stories on the new partnership. It was news because Dizzy, a celebrity on the world stage, left a huge record company to start a very risky venture, and also because he was making the deal with an unknown white Jewish guy with little experience in the record business. The coverage gave us credibility and opened doors to distributors. Ultimately, we had 28 distributors.

Left to right: Eddie Bierman, one of my lifelong friends, Dizzy, and me, at the first recording session of Dee Gee at United Sound Systems Recording Studios in Detroit in 1951.

We recorded at Jimmy and Joe Siracuse's United Sound Systems studio in Detroit where I had spent considerable time learning the business. We recorded on a German-manufactured Ampex Model No. 354 which, at the time, was state-of-the-art equipment. Despite its bulkiness — it weighed about 300 pounds, standing four feet tall, two feet wide and more than two feet deep — it produced a very high sound quality. I still have an Ampex 354 in my apartment in Detroit; it is valued memorabilia from a bygone era.

The first Dee Gee recording featured two compositions: "Tin Tin Deo" and "Birks Works." Other pieces recorded later included: "We Love to Boogie," with vocals by Freddie Strong and the Calypso Boys, "School Days," "Oo-Shoo-Bee-Doo-Bee," "Lady Be Good," and "Umbrella Man." Other numbers that made it big were "The Champ," a very moving rendition of "Stardust," and "Caravan."

Dizzy worked with some of the best musicians at the time, including: John Coltrane, tenor and alto sax; Kenny Burrell, guitar; Percy Heath, bass; Kansas Fields, drums; and Milt Jackson, vibes.

Given his humorous streak, Dizzy composed a song called "Swing Low, Sweet Cadillac," which was sung to the music of the very moving spiritual, "Swing Low, Sweet Chariot." The lyrics:

> *Swing Low, Sweet Cadillac*
> *Comin' for to carry me home;*
> *Swing Low, Sweet Cadillac,*
> *Comin' for to carry me home.*

> *I looked over Jordan, and what did I see?*
> *Comin' for to carry me home,*
> *O, an Eldorado, comin' after me,*
> *Comin' for to carry me home.*

The song concludes:

> *Old Cadillacs never die,*
> *The finance company just fade 'em away.*

39

To increase our opportunities for sales and profit, I suggested to Dizzy that we record other musicians. Why limit ourselves? Given Dizzy's reputation, I felt that other artists would be very eager to record with Dee Gee. He agreed, and we expanded our operations. A primary objective, as Dizzy said at the time, was to bring the non-jazz public into the jazz orbit. Many of the artists we recorded made their debut with Dee Gee, and later achieved worldwide fame. In all, Dee Gee produced 36 singles.

Other artists that we recorded were members of the Milt Jackson Quartet which included: John Lewis, piano; Milt Jackson, vibraphone; Percy Heath and Ray Brown, bass; and Kenny Clarke drums. The quartet would become world-famous as the Modern Jazz Quartet (it ultimately changed its name to MJQ), and it owed its beginnings to Dee Gee.

We moved quickly to expand our market. We recruited, among others: Shelly Manne, drums; Milton "Shorty" Rogers, trumpet and flugelhorn; Secondo "Conte" Candoli, trumpet; Annie Ross, vocalist; Art Pepper, saxophone and clarinet; Blossom Dearie, vocalist and piano; and Bill Russo, trombone and arranger, who had worked with the band leader, Stan Kenton.

In addition, we recorded Billy Mitchell, tenor sax; Barry Harris, piano; as well as Thad Jones, trumpet; and his brother Elvin, drums. With another brother, Hank, on piano, they made up the famous Jones Brothers. They were from Pontiac, Michigan, about 30 miles north of Detroit.

We also recorded the fantastic blues singer Sonny Boy Wilson (later known as Jackie Wilson) who was unknown at the time. When he took his paycheck from Dee Gee to buy shoes in a downtown Detroit store, I was called to vouch for the check. A few years later, when Wilson became a star around the world, the store owner would have loved to have Wilson as a customer, and probably would have given him the shoes free just for the publicity.

A major challenge was keeping up with the continual changes in recording equipment. The technology in the manufacturing of records improved quickly, moving from the lathe, which imprinted records, to wire — a method that didn't last long — and finally tape. With the new technology, we produced three LPs (long playing) that had six to eight selections on them. At the time, this was pioneering stuff.

Not all of Dizzy's numbers were pure bebop. Some of the records featured blues, rhythm and pop, and Dizzy was criticized for going "too commercial." He was offended by this reaction because one of our objectives was to reach more music lovers, particularly those unfamiliar with jazz. Jazz had a limited audience at the time and we wanted to broaden our appeal. That was Dee Gee's primary objective, so we produced a broad range of music and even humor to achieve our goal. In pursuing these objectives, we did nothing to sacrifice the talents of the musicians. We made sure that the musicians could express themselves as they always had. Sure, there were what we called "moldy figs" in the music business, people who were so conservative that they could not accept anything they considered unorthodox.

Dee Gee was struggling financially when I made a terrible mistake which led to its demise. Let's just say I was a *schmuck, a putt.* These words are off-color pejoratives (they mean "penis" in Yiddish.) They also mean "dumb" and "stupid." And I was all of that.

I was introduced to Herman Lubinsky, who operated Savoy Records out of Newark, New Jersey. He produced blues, jazz and gospel records, and he was interested in becoming our major distributor. I had been warned that Lubinsky was a *goniff* (thief, scoundrel), and that he really had no passion for or even interest in jazz; he was just interested in profits. Some people said he had contempt for black musicians.

Kofsky wrote the following about Lubinsky in his book, *Black Music, White Business*:

"Savoy's owner made no pretense whatsoever of regarding black music as art; to him it was merely a commodity, something that could be sold for a profit just like any other item in the stock.

"Lubinsky's contempt for black music, its artists, and its audience, emerged… in a multitude of ways. Most revealing of all, though, was his unwillingness to develop any understanding — appreciation, of course was entirely out of the question — of the art that brought him such lucrative returns."

I had several discussions with Lubinsky and, ignoring the warnings I was given, I signed an agreement with him at the Palmer House in Chicago where we were attending a convention. The contract for a 10-year lease was handwritten by Lubinsky's attorney and I signed it. Then Lubinsky asked me for sheets of my stationery with my signature at the bottom. He said he would write letters to our distributors, informing them of our lease agreement, over my signature.

I don't know what he wrote in those letters, but it wasn't long before we had serious financial problems. We owed taxes, some invoices weren't being paid, and the end result was that in 1953, a little more than 2½ years after we launched the label, we were almost broke. The government, given our tax problems, seized the masters of our recordings and worked out a deal with Lubinsky. Lubinsky continued to operate Dee Gee for about another 10 years without any involvement from Dizzy or me.

As I said, I acted stupidly, and I still cannot believe I was so naïve. I felt terrible, and took full responsibility for the failure. When I told Dizzy what I had done, he never chastised me for my stupidity. He never said one critical word.

I know that some books on Dizzy and other reports blamed Dee Gee's failure entirely on our delinquent taxes. They state that despite my responsibilities to run the business, I failed to pay the taxes. That is just not true. Yes, we were late in paying them. In fact, at one point the IRS threatened to confiscate my car. After some negotiations, we worked it out, and all the taxes were paid. The primary reason for Dee Gee's failure was, to repeat, my naiveté in signing a lease agreement with Lubinsky.

After Lubinsky took over, Savoy released "Dizzy Gillespie Dee Gee Days, the Savoy Collection" which was an album of work Dizzy and I produced. Michael G. Nastos, a highly respected jazz music critic, called it, "One of the most important albums in jazz history and belongs in every serious — and whimsical — jazz lover's collection — period!"

On the "good news" side, Lubinsky, who died in 1974, taught me an important business lesson: Don't be too quick to trust others. True, it led to some cynicism on my part, and in the next 60 years as a businessman, I was probably more careful at times than I needed to be. But as they say, better safe than...

The crisis led to the only major disagreement that Dizzy and I ever had. Recognizing that we were facing severe financial difficulties, Dizzy recorded a piece with Roulette, a company run by Morris Levy and Teddy Reig, major producers of jazz between 1940 and 1960. Dizzy was still my partner in Dee Gee, and when I found out, I was angry. I called Dizzy on the phone and cussed him out. I told him that I had put up all the money, and did all the organizational work. I accused him, most importantly, of undermining our friendship. I was furious; I didn't mince any words, using profanity. When I finished venting my anger, I could hear Dizzy cry. He understood that he had violated a business agreement and, even worse, betrayed a trust, my trust.

After we cleared the air, Dizzy acknowledged his mistake, and we moved on. As Leslie Gourse said in her book, *Dizzy Gillespie and the Birth of Bebop*, (she was not addressing the fight between Dizzy and me) friends may go through terrible disappointments but their love survive[s].

Gourse was right. Our friendship not only survived but, happily, it thrived.

MY ROAD TO BECOMING
AN ENVIRONMENTALIST

6

—●—

The failure of Dee Gee was a huge disappointment. Our hopes had been high, but given all the pressures, particularly the financial ones, it was not a total surprise.

I launched a couple of other labels; both were short-lived. First came Prize in a partnership with Bob Maxwell, a Detroit DJ. We produced only one record with Little Willie John, a new R&B (rhythm and blues) vocalist. Then I created Sugar Hill, but our output was only two 78s of gospel music featuring The Five Scalders.

Thus, I turned more attention and focus to my other career: the oil recycling and related businesses that my father and brother, Morris, continued to nurture. I had never left the business even when running Dee Gee. I continued working for my father and brother when time permitted. They humored me and kept me involved, hoping that I would lose interest in jazz. One day, they thought, if they kept me busy at Usher Oil (my father had changed the name of the company from Usher Waste Oil Service to Usher Oil), I would come to my senses and devote all my energies to a "responsible" money-making endeavor. Eventually, they believed, I would give up my jazz *meshugas* (craziness). Hope springs eternal, especially for parents who believe their child is heading down the wrong path.

Although my father and brother had doubts about my interest in the oil recycling business, I worked hard at Usher Oil. At one point, I recommended a new process for cleaning oil called "centrifuging." This new development provided a process for removing foreign particles from oil, and it permitted us to clean oil faster as well as clean it more effectively.

After the typical family-business arguments about ideas I put on the table, my father and brother agreed, primarily because they recognized that we were facing tough, sophisticated competition. I said we needed to buy new equipment. We made the financial investment and bought new larger tanks, tanks 50 feet in diameter which had the capacity to hold a half million gallons of oil. We also needed new heating equipment to help with the flow of oil, and I became the boiler operator.

I had read about two companies in Philadelphia that manufactured equipment for ships to remove water and sediment from lubricants. I called one of them, and it agreed to help us achieve our objectives. At the same time, my father and brother bought another business, Michigan Tank Cleaning, and I was assigned to run that operation. We cleaned tanks after barges unloaded their cargos, and the storage facilities had to be especially clean because the ships sometimes loaded cargos different from those they delivered. We cleaned tanks on ships where I had picked up oil near the Detroit River about a year earlier.

Detroit was becoming a port with heavy ship traffic, primarily because the St. Lawrence Seaway had been expanded. Shipping also increased on the Detroit River as a result of a strike in Montreal. The strike forced ships to unload in Detroit and then transport cargo to its destination by rail. Some of these ships carried tallow: animal renderings. I recognized that these ships needed to have clean tanks which provided us with another major business opportunity.

I formed my own company, Marine Services Corp., and I made Morris a full partner. I created a logo, a red anchor, which I would use for years, both for my non-music career and, in later years, for my business in jazz. As much as I would like to take credit for the logo, a sketch of it came from a friend,

Bob Carrington, who was a news and movie announcer at WXYZ-TV, Channel 7, an ABC affiliate in Detroit.

I made inroads on the docks very quickly. I noticed that the ships would hire unskilled workers off the streets to clean the tanks. They didn't look very professional. So, I bought my employees blue overalls and helmets, had my logo imprinted on both, and when my men showed up at the docks, the ships' officers were impressed by their appearance. This opened many doors for my company, and we expanded quickly, and even offered carpentry work to brace and block military tanks, automobiles, trucks, and locomotives.

We cleaned the tanks of the ships while they were "riding the hook" — anchored in the river waiting for a berth. My men would also "ride the ships" — travel with them and clean empty tanks as the ships headed toward their next destinations.

Occasionally, we cleaned up small oil spills as well as hazardous materials. Concerns about the environment were not yet in the public consciousness, but two events changed all of that, and prompted me to think about another possible line of business: cleaning up oil pollution on the water.

The first event was the publication of a book, *Silent Spring*, by Rachel Carson in 1962. Published by Houghton Mifflin, the book warned about the use of pesticides and their impact on birds and the environment. Carson claimed that chemical companies were disingenuous in their public statements about the dangers of pesticides, and that government officials were not adopting appropriate policies to protect the environment. The book made headlines throughout the U.S., and raised public awareness about pollution.

The second event was the shipwreck of a supertanker, the *Torrey Canyon*, off the western coast of Cornwall, England in 1967. The tanker, owned by the Barracuda Tanker Corporation, a subsidiary of Union Oil Company of California, and operated by British Petroleum, was the largest vessel ever involved in such a wreck. The ship, carrying 110,000 tons of oil, struck a reef and was grounded, causing an environmental disaster.

Carson's book and the shipwreck had a huge impact on the public, igniting concerns about protecting our fragile environment. The media fanned the flames, so to speak, with their coverage of the book and the disaster on the high seas. I had been thinking of launching a new business devoted to cleaning up polluted waters, and these events heightened my interest. I began doing research into what I needed to do to initiate such an endeavor.

Then came a telephone call that settled the issue. Officials at the Ford Motor Co.'s Rouge Plant called, asking if I could clean up a spill of some 20,000 gallons of oil on the Rouge River. They had heard that I was a "troubleshooter" of sorts on the waterfront on problems like this, and asked me to help them.

"Bring your navy," they pleaded frantically.

I didn't hesitate, although I must admit I didn't exactly know how I would handle the crisis. Whatever equipment I had wasn't designed to clean up oil spills. I improvised, using vacuum trucks and making mechanical alterations on other vehicles so I could use them as well. For absorbents, I spread straw, and I had some very primitive dispersants available. Ford had only one boom, from the UK, to contain the oil, and it cost an unbelievable $45 a foot. We did manage to find a boom called "slickbar" in the U.S. The assignment from Ford was my first purchase order for an environmental cleanup, and we were to do more work for Ford in the years to come.

As we were working on the spill, I discussed creating a company specifically devoted to oil and hazardous material cleanup with a friend, Bert Piggott, who was operating a company, J.T. Wing. He was a ship chandler, a provider to ships of supplies such as food, liquor, cigarettes, bedding and hardware. I asked if he were interested in becoming a partner in my proposed venture. He agreed, but added that he had serious time constraints. Given the limited commitment he could make, he proposed a 60-40 split, with me receiving the 60 percent. Piggott was a very honest man.

Silent Spring, the *Torrey Canyon* disaster, the accident on the Rouge River, and the changing political landscape all led to the establishment of Marine Pollution Control (MPC) in August 1967. I filed incorporation papers for MPC in April 1968, and transferred the red anchor logo from Marine Services to MPC.

At the beginning our offices, like the branch offices of Dee Gee, were at Usher Oil. Five years later, we moved to the edge of the Rouge River, just west of Livernois on Detroit's lower west side in an area known as Delray. MPC has been headquartered there ever since.

I believe that the MPC property should be proclaimed an historic site by the government. In 1925, during the Prohibition Era, a family named Nykiel constructed the building for one purpose: to store illegal booze delivered at night from Canada in Chris-Craft and Gar Wood speed boats.

These boats would race across the Detroit River and dock in boat wells, out of sight, under the building. The boat wells were located right under what later became my offices. The booze would be unloaded, stored and then trucks sent by the mobster Al Capone would pick it up for delivery to Chicago. I assume there were other customers besides Capone. I heard these stories from eye witnesses, including the owner of the property, Captain Frank Becker, from whom I bought the building, and also a Nykiel family member who was a classmate of my wife, Althea. "Nykiel" and the year the building was constructed — 1925 — are inscribed in the façade above what was once an entrance to the building.

I never had any firsthand knowledge of this story until, while doing research for this book, Berl Falbaum, my co-author, and I found a Nykiel family member, Edward Nykiel, of Grosse Ile, Michigan, who told us that the building was constructed by his grandfather, August J. "Gus" Nykiel. Gus Nykiel, a veteran of World War I, he said, had a house in Canada and ran boats back and forth across the Detroit River. Edward Nykiel said his grandfather was a powerful individual in the Detroit area community, owning a semi-professional football team named, like the city's pro baseball team, the Detroit Tigers — and he was a prominent as well as generous philanthropist.

Gus Nykiel owned a pool hall and a saloon that served as the headquarters for his bootlegging operation at 8824 West Jefferson, a short walk from my offices — the building he constructed — at 8631 West Jefferson. When Gus Nykiel was only 32, he was assassinated on June 27, 1928 by two organized crime figures in a confrontation in front of the saloon. He had one of the largest funerals ever witnessed in the Detroit area.

MPC became a pioneer in a new business, and it was among the first companies to be designated as an official oil spill control company by the U.S. Coast Guard. We helped develop equipment and techniques in oil spill control and own 14 patents. We built two boats — *Buda I* and *Buda II* — that were designed specifically for skimming oil off water surfaces.

"Buda" was comprised of the first two letters of my partner's first name, "Burt", and the first two letters of "Dave." I made one little mistake: after we had the names painted on the boats, I learned my partner spelled "Burt" with an "e."

At the time I was writing this book, MPC was working on the development of a two-man submarine — STAR (Submerged Transport & Recovery) — which would clean up oil at the bottom of oceans, lakes and rivers, up to a depth of 720 feet.

The concept for a submarine had its origin from my days of working for my father as a truck driver, spreading oil on gravel roads to control dust. Now I wanted to retrieve oil. When divers walked on the bottoms of bodies of water to recover sunken oil, their movements would disturb the oil, causing it to rise and block their vision. To solve this problem, I proposed the development of a submarine.

For almost a half century, MPC has assisted in cleaning up some of the world's worst oil spills, including the 1989 Exxon Valdez spill in Alaska and the Persian Gulf in 1991, when the Iraqi dictator, Saddam Hussein, dumped millions of gallons of oil into the Gulf. Without sounding self-serving, I think we have made important contributions to the protection of the environment. We also helped develop government policies relating to oil spills, with officeholders seeking our counsel and advice, and we have testified periodically before Congress. The first major legislation regarding the transport of oil on the water and related issues was not adopted at the federal level until 1970; few local communities had any controls.

As to MPC, I credit my ability to launch the company to my experience at the Farragut Academy, visiting the Coast Guard station in Charlevoix, my membership in the YSA, and the Coast Guard Reserve. Each played a part in giving me the foundation to deal with problems ships encounter with such crises as oil spills on and below the water.

Simply put, I evolved to become an environmentalist (that development, I might add, started when I was five years old when I already worked with my father) and launched a new international business. Of course, I never abandoned my first love, the world of jazz, much to the consternation of my father and brother. My two careers never overlapped although, in 1984, I did appoint Dizzy to the Marine Pollution Control Board of Directors.

DIZZY TOURS
SOUTH AMERICA, 1956

7

As I wrote in the previous chapter, the downfall of Dee Gee was a terrible disappointment, of course, but I learned important lessons about the record industry and also, as I indicated, about being a little more careful in business, especially in making judgments about whom to trust. Yes, I learned the latter lesson the hard way, and it proved invaluable in future years.

Most of my time now was spent working for my father, but I made a point of seeing Dizzy as often as I could. I frequently flew to New York or other cities where he performed. I was very conscious of the fact that I was living in two very separate worlds: One in the waste oil business and the other in jazz. Frequently, the flight paths of planes I took out of Detroit Metropolitan Airport would take me over the routes I drove as a truck driver for my father. I was not ignorant of the contrasts between my diverse interests. And I did sympathize, a little bit anyway, with my father's concerns about my compulsion with jazz and that, at times, I was leaving him when he needed me. The problem was that I was never able to shake off my irresistible love of jazz.

When I caught up with Dizzy at the clubs where he performed, I served as his confidant. He asked me to check staging, microphones, lighting and, if the sessions were recorded, to assure that the sound systems were functioning at peak performance.

I also served as what is called in the business an "A&R"— artist and repertoire — man in recording sessions. I provided Dizzy and the band feedback during their rehearsals as well as public performances. Sometimes the pieces may have lacked passion or emotion which is so important in jazz since much of it is improvisation. It was a role that I also played at Emanon, Dee Gee, Prize, Sugar Hill, and Argo, a division of Chess Records, which I would join in 1958.

It's true that I had no technical skills in music. I could not read music, I was not a musician, and my background, as I indicated, was in classical music. But I had an inherent talent to distinguish mediocre jazz from jazz that moved people. Dizzy and the musicians recognized my abilities and I had their respect.

Of course, I had to be careful how I offered my critiques. After all, the members of Dizzy's band included some of the most talented musicians in the world and, in many cases, I was dealing with immense egos. I would never simply state, "You should really play it this way." They were, after all, the masters. I was extremely careful in making suggestions. Sometimes I would recommend they replay a number because the recording equipment had failed. At other times, I would claim that the solo by a saxophonist or trumpet player did not come through clearly.

An A&R man is a vital member of the team, and thus has a responsibility to be as honest as possible. My job was to make sure the music had a healthy pregnancy, so to speak, and then birth. The obligation of an A&R man is to help create the proper mood, excitement and exhilaration in the music. He has to work to produce the best possible atmosphere in which to record. In jazz, that means making sure that the musicians create the "feel" that is so important. I had a responsibility and obligation to bring out their talent as best as I could. Who offered the opinion was not the issue. The issue was that I had to do what was necessary to get the best out of them. It wasn't about me; it was about the music.

Frankly, I don't believe anyone was fooled by my efforts at diplomacy. The musicians recognized my role as the A&R man for Dizzy. I had created trusting relationships, and I always valued the respect the band had for the feedback I offered.

Occasionally, a member of the band was annoyed and challenged my assessments. Those challenges usually came from those who had problems with alcohol or drugs. Some were argumentative by nature, and I had to deal with them differently. Overall, I didn't encounter many problems. Of course, everyone recognized that I had no ulterior motive. We all had the same objective which was to produce the best recordings possible. Why else would I offer any criticism?

This role as A&R advisor also strengthened my relationship with Dizzy. He appreciated that I had the ability to critique the pieces, and that I tried very hard not to create ill feelings. As always, we were of one mind; as I have indicated, we were brothers.

During one visit to New York, Dizzy asked me to join him on a tour of South America sponsored by the U.S. State Department. The idea was to showcase jazz music and, because the band was integrated, to have the musicians serve as ambassadors to indicate how progressive the U.S. was in race relations. Dizzy had completed another such trip through the Middle East and considered it so effective that, as reported in books about Dizzy, he had written President Eisenhower stating:

"Our trip through the Middle East proved conclusively that our interracial group was powerfully effective against Red propaganda. Jazz is our own American folk music that communicates with all peoples regardless of language barriers."

Actually, Dizzy wanted me to accompany him to the Middle East but decided that a Jew on that trip would not be conducive to forging better relations with some of the countries on the itinerary. The State Department agreed, and I was replaced as a liaison on the Middle East trip by Marshall Stearns, a jazz buff, writer, and professor at several U.S. colleges.

I was approved by the State Department for the South American trip, and was even given a special designation. I would be the public information officer (PIO.) As the PIO, I had no official duties. I didn't have to do anything except, periodically, report to the various consulates on the progress of the tour and communicate any problems we might have encountered. Each time we visited an embassy or were visited by officials, I was a major contact.

A productive relationship with the various embassies was essential because I would need their help with technical issues such as finding the proper electrical converters, magnetic tape and other key equipment I would need to record the sessions. The officials were very supportive because they wanted the trip to succeed.

A powerful politician who was principally responsible for making these tours a reality was the African-American congressman from Harlem, Adam Clayton Powell, Jr., the first black from New York to be elected to the U.S. House of Representatives. He continually pressured President Eisenhower and the State Department to sponsor such tours, arguing that trips abroad featuring classical music and ballet were not productive in achieving the desired objectives of demonstrating America's commitment to human equality. Instead, he proposed the U.S. sponsor tours of jazz artists.

As reported by *Americana, the Journal of American Popular Culture*, Powell told reporters, "I am going to propose to President Eisenhower that he sent this man (Gillespie), who's a great contributor to our music, on a State Department sponsored cultural mission to Africa, the Near East, Middle East and Asia." Powell was married to Hazel Dorothy Scott, an internationally acclaimed jazz singer and classical pianist.

Technically, the tour was being conducted under the auspices of the American National Theater Academy (ANTA), a quasi-governmental, non-profit organization created by law in 1935 to be the official representative agency for U.S. theater. A major responsibility of the organization was to sponsor tours to foreign countries.

Dizzy wanted me on the trip primarily to record the concerts on a new portable machine, an Ampex Model No. 600. The Ampex 600 was much less bulky than previous models and could be carried in two Samsonite suitcases. The machine was specifically designed so it could be transported easily without sacrificing quality. As an incentive, Dizzy said he and Lorraine would pay me for the trip and they did, and I always considered this a very kind gesture on their part. They weren't making big bucks.

Admittedly, whether or not to join the tour was a difficult personal decision on two fronts. First, I would have to leave my job and tell my father I was going on what he would consider another jazz junket. This was no easy task since my jazz interest continued to be an irritant to him and my brother, his partner. Second, I would have to tell my wife, Althea. At the time, we had been married only two years and already had one of our four children. As I was struggling with the professional and personal conflicts, the magnetic force of joining this trip was too much to resist. I made the decision to join Dizzy, and my usual role as a producer changed to engineer. (My wife and I had five children: Lisa, Ellen, Amy, Charlie, and Billie, who died at the age of two months. We divorced after 23 years of marriage in 1977.)

At the time, Dizzy was under contract with Norman Granz, a jazz impresario, promoter and producer who ran an organization called Jazz at the Philharmonic. For some reason, I don't know why, Granz never had any interest in the music Dizzy would produce on this trip.

Including travel, the trip would run 23 days and our schedule was as follows: Ecuador July 26-27; Buenos Aires, Argentina July 28-August 4; Montevideo, Uruguay August 5; Rio de Janeiro, Brazil August 6-12; and São Paulo, Brazil August 13-17.

I flew from Detroit to New York where we caught a plane to Guayaquil, a port city in Ecuador. We then traveled to Quito, the capital, for a concert, and returned to Guayaquil for another engagement. The receptions were phenomenal with huge crowds welcoming Dizzy because he had a world reputation. They loved jazz and they loved Dizzy, and Dizzy loved them.

The band was comprised of 17 musicians, including four white artists and a black woman, Melba Liston, who played the trombone and was also an arranger. In addition to Dizzy and Liston, the band included these black musicians: Quincy Jones, Bama Warwick, E.V. Perry, and Joe Gordon, all on trumpet; Jimmy Powell, alto sax; Benny Golson and Billy Mitchell, tenor sax; Walter Davis Jr., piano; Nelson Boyd, bass; and Charlie Persip, drums. In addition, there was the baritone vocalist, Austin Cromer. The white musicians were: Phil Woods, alto sax; Frank Rehak and Rod Levitt, trombone; and Marty Flax, baritone sax. A fifth white musician, Lalo Schifrin, piano, joined us during the tour.

In Quito, Joe Gordon griped that he was not given a chance to be in the spotlight, and maintained that he was as good on the trumpet as Dizzy. Quincy Jones told me that when Dizzy heard about the complaints, he said that in the upcoming performance Gordon could play "A Night in Tunisia." There was a method to Dizzy's madness.

Quito is more than 9,000 feet above sea level, the highest capital in the world, and the entire band was having trouble breathing. The high altitude was particularly hard on the guys playing wind instruments — trumpets, saxophones and trombones. It was tough. "A Night in Tunisia" is almost nine minutes long and requires tremendous lung power and breath control. Gordon played "Tunisia" that night in the thin air of Quito, and, in doing so, almost fell off the bandstand. As Jones said in different venues, Gordon almost killed himself.

In Guayaquil, Gordon became very ill from drug use. We needed to get him home, and the responsibility fell on my shoulders. I made sure that Gordon got on a plane back to the U.S. while the band continued on. Then I flew and caught up with Dizzy and the band. If Gordon had stayed, given the lesson he learned in Quito, I doubt that he would have complained again. As Jones said when he told me the story, "Dizzy is so smart…the fox that he is." Gordon was replaced by Franco Corvini, an Argentinean trumpet player.

Dizzy assigned Jones, who had been on previous tours with Dizzy, to be in charge of rehearsals when Dizzy wasn't able to do so. Jones handled the rehearsals, especially when the band was to play one of his arrangements. Jones was only 23 years old and he was very flattered that Dizzy would trust him with that responsibility. Jones tells the story that Billy Mitchell, tenor sax, told him, "I like you, but you're too young to take orders from…I can't handle that." Jones just laughed and responded, "That's fair enough."

From Ecuador, we flew to Buenos Aires in what became, for us, the longest one-nighter in history. We had to fly 2,700 miles from Ecuador, which is in northwestern South America, to the southeastern tip of the continent, and play that very night. That was one helluva long trip by plane at that time.

What's more, as we were flying over the Andes, the plane lost two of its four engines, and we flew for about two hours on just two engines. Surprisingly, there was no panic on the plane, although many of us suddenly became very religious, and prayed that God would forgive our sins — and given the group involved, that was a big request — and let us land safely. We were scheduled to land at Ezeiza Airport in Buenos Aires at 8 p.m.; we arrived at about 10:30 p.m.

Our welcoming party had been informed of the plane's mechanical problems by the pilot, and word spread quickly throughout the city with the media reporting on our travail. In addition, the audience in the concert hall had been told we would be late, and that they would have to wait. And wait they did in the Teatro Casino. We didn't arrive at the casino until after midnight because protocol required that we first check in at our hotel where we had to leave our passports at the registration desk. The patience and determination of the audience to stay for the performance was a testimonial to Dizzy's reputation. We arrived to a thunderous ovation, and I don't think there was an empty seat in the house.

After the concert, we learned of another snag, one that had serious international political and diplomatic implications and consequences. We had been told that we would be staying at the Savoy, a U.S.-owned hotel, but our hosts took us to the Continental Hotel. None of us understood why the change had been made, but we asked no questions.

We learned later that the Savoy had refused to provide rooms for us. Why? Because most of the musicians were black. Talk about irony. Here was a tour designed to showcase the liberal racial policies of the U.S., its progressiveness in inter-racial relations, in the hope of improving such relations around the world, and one of our first experiences was to face blatant discrimination.

When they learned of Savoy's bigotry, the band members were understandably upset. Of course, they also recognized that blacks still faced similar discrimination in the U.S., particularly in the South. If they had spoken out, the Savoy and its supporters might very well have responded that they acted no differently than many similar establishments in the U.S. Thus, the band members did not vent their anger or protest publicly. They also recognized their role as ambassadors of the U.S. and didn't want to cause an "international incident."

Interestingly, someone who was very upset was the former president of Notre Dame University, the Rev. Dr. Theodore Hesburgh, who was a passenger on our plane and had played chess with Dizzy during the journey. He was staying at the Savoy and when he learned about the ban, he was beside himself particularly, he told us, after he saw a sheik with a goat on the hotel's elevator.

I found out about the Savoy's actions from a reporter, Peter Hahn, a CBS stringer, while I was setting up my recording equipment in the theater. Since I was the PIO, he kept asking me for my reaction to the Savoy's discriminatory act. I responded, "I don't know what the hell you're talking about." I was under pressure to set up, and finally told him I would talk to him when

Dizzy and me relaxing during the 1956 U.S.-sponsored tour of South America.

my job was completed. When I finished, he told me why we were forced to change hotels and that the story was spreading quickly in the media. It was creating what we now call a "media frenzy." Sure enough, the story was published throughout South America but not in the U.S.

Hahn took me under his wing, stating he would give me a lesson on how the reporting system worked in that part of the world. For that lesson, we went to *La Prensa*, the city's daily newspaper. The paper's building, incidentally, was pockmarked with bullet holes from battles fought only a few weeks earlier between various political factions. At *La Prensa*, Hahn sent a story containing information from the local papers on the Savoy incident to New York using the Associated Press wire, and explained to me that before it would be published in the U.S., it would be returned to us in Spanish. The story, however, never came back. It had been killed. I don't know if the story was "spiked" by Argentinean authorities, the U.S. State Department or the U.S. media. Whatever happened, the American public never learned of the outrage, at least not from our media institutions. Not a word was published in the U.S. It was a *schande* (shame.)

This made me even more cynical about the world than I already was. I was never naïve, but this taught me another lesson that I would not soon forget. I had a new appreciation of how power is wielded, and that in most instances, we don't know who is making the decisions — or why.

Dizzy was angry that word never reached the U.S., but what were we going to do? We didn't want to stir the political pot, so to speak; nonetheless, we were deeply disappointed about the blackout. The incident embarrassed the Argentinean administration, and the president, Pedro Aramburu, contacted ANTA, the national academy sponsoring the trip, asking if Dizzy would come to the Casa Rosada (Pink House), the executive mansion and office of the president of Argentina, the equivalent of our White House. President Aramburu said he wanted to apologize to Dizzy on behalf of his country. Aramburu, a former Army general, had taken over as president only about 8 1/2 months earlier after helping to depose the dictator, Juan Perón.

Dizzy was sleeping when the call came so I represented him, and Hahn — we had become good friends by now — accompanied me. It happened very quickly. I didn't even have time to shave. The President was very effusive in his apology, stating he was embarrassed by the incident which did not, in any way, reflect the policies of his government.

I was polite and thanked him for his thoughtfulness. I said I was pleased to accept the apology on behalf of Mr. Gillespie and the band. I said I would relay the apology to Mr. Gillespie, and told the President that I was confident Mr. Gillespie would appreciate his sensitivity. President Aramburu told me the Savoy had been fined $2,500.

As each of us tried to deal with the bigotry of the Savoy incident, a major positive by-product of our trip to Argentina was that, by happenstance, it opened the doors for a musician who would become world famous: Lalo Schifrin, in whose future I played an indirect role.

In Buenos Aires, as in the United States, we always ran into fans who wanted to shake hands or get autographs from band members, particularly Dizzy. In the U.S. these fans are sometimes called "groupies;" in our world of music we called them "nails." It was actually an affectionate term and referred to the fact that once they got a hold of you, they wouldn't let go. They had you "nailed." In using the word, we did not intend any animus. In Argentina, "nails" would stand in the hotel hallways outside the rooms.

One day, I ran into Schifrin, who already had established an excellent reputation as a pianist, composer and conductor in Argentina. He had the only big bebop band in the country. He wanted to meet Dizzy because, as he has stated in books and articles years later, Dizzy was his idol. He once told me, "I had many teachers, but only one master." Seeing me coming in and out of rooms, he concluded that I was part of the band's inner circle, and asked if I would take him to Dizzy. He had a musical composition in his hands.

"Please, please, I must see Mr. Gillespie," he pleaded. "I have a manuscript I want to give him."

Schifrin told me he had met Dizzy a day or two before at a club, the Rendezvous Porteño, where Schifrin was playing. Dizzy asked Schifrin who had arranged the music. When Schifrin replied he had, Dizzy invited him to move to the U.S.*

In the hallway of our hotel, Schifrin, clutching his composition in his hands, told me he wanted to show Dizzy an arrangement he had written. I concluded that Schifrin wanted to pursue the conversation he had with Dizzy at the Rendezvous Porteño. I thought his story was credible; I did not consider him a "nail" so I took him in to see Dizzy.

Dizzy immediately remembered Schifrin and repeated how impressed he was by Schifrin's talent, and invited him to join us on the tour, which he did. After our return to the States, at Dizzy's earlier invitation, Schifrin came to New York where Dizzy gave him a job as a piano player in the band. In 1960, four years after the tour, Dizzy commissioned him to write a piece, and Schifrin composed the five-part "Gillespiana Suite."

Regarding "Gillespiana," Schifrin says in the liner notes of the CD:

"As soon as I had joined Dizzy Gillespie's band, he said, 'Why don't you write something for us?' His words triggered my imagination, and the ideas started to flow. Diz had been one of my greatest inspirations (still is), and the composition process was intense and exhilarating.

"A few days later, I took the sketches of 'Gillespiana' to his home and played them on the piano. When I finished, he asked me, 'How are you going to orchestrate this work?' I replied, 'I hear a jazz quintet... plus a brass band.' Diz immediately called Norman Granz who was, at that time, the head of Verve Records. With the telephone in his hand, he asked me how long it would take to arrange it. 'Three weeks,' was my response. He told Norman, 'Book a studio a month from now.' And this is how 'Gillespiana' was born..."

Schifrin's relationship with Dizzy opened doors for him in Hollywood. He is best known for composing the famous theme song for "Mission Impossible." He did much more. He won four Grammy Awards, received six Oscar nominations, was the recipient of numerous music awards, and worked

---

*I learned later that Schifrin actually had met Dizzy in 1953 when Dizzy was performing in Paris where Schifrin was studying.

with actor Clint Eastwood in the Dirty Harry movies. Among Schifrin's big hits were "Bullitt," "Cool Hand Luke," "Tango," "Rush Hour," and "The Amityville Horror."

While Lalo Schifrin obviously wasn't a "nail" in the true meaning of the word, there was one, a Catholic priest, Father John Crowley, who fit all of the word's nuances. He was a priest from Boston assigned to a church in Paraguay. He had read about Dizzy's visit to Argentina and flew down to meet him.

I saw him in the hall, dressed in a robe, and he told me, "I'm a Redemptorist [Jesuit] stationed in Paraguay. I heard on the radio about you people playing here, and I came over to hear Dizzy. I used to play jazz saxophone." I arranged a meeting for him with Dizzy. Interestingly, he became a counselor to Dizzy's wife who was Catholic, and the two frequently engaged in long conversations. What's more, I don't know how he traveled, but he showed up at several of our stops in South America, and a "loose" relationship continued in the States. He was a very committed "nail."

We had an unplanned but very pleasant experience when Dizzy was approached by Argentina's king of the tango, Osvaldo Fresedo, who asked Dizzy if he would record some pieces at Fresedo's club, the Rendezvous Porteño, the same club at which Schifrin met Dizzy. Dizzy graciously accepted, which led to a somewhat embarrassing PR event that I had planned. I wanted the most coverage I could get for Dizzy's appearance, so I planned to have Dizzy arrive on horseback in a gaucho outfit, which Hahn reported publicly.

With Hahn's help, I managed to obtain a gaucho costume from a local opera house. They had hundreds of costumes, of course, for the characters in operas, and they were glad to help. I still needed a horse. I found a riding stable near the airport. They had a horse, but no way to transport it. It would have to be ridden.

No problem, I said. I would take a taxi and a stable boy would ride the horse behind me. I looked at the horse and it was so mangy, I didn't even know if we would make it to the club which was about 10 miles from the stable.

The scene was incredible. Here we were moving at about five-six miles an hour through heavy traffic. Somehow, we made it. Dizzy, already dressed as a gaucho, mounted the horse. In one hand, he had his trumpet and, in the other, the reins along with a glass of milk. The media and hundreds of Argentineans watched.

Then Dizzy made a little mistake. At least I think it was a mistake. He touched the horse lightly with his spurs. This nag, that I thought might drop dead on the way to the club, went wild. It took off, racing and dodging between cars on an eight-lane main thoroughfare, with me and others trying to corral it. I don't know how Dizzy stayed on the horse. We finally managed to catch the horse and Dizzy wasn't hurt. The incident created huge headlines. Dizzy was unfazed, went into the club and played, in his gaucho outfit, for more than an hour with Fresedo's band, and the jam session created a warm friendship between Dizzy, Fresedo, who died in 1984, and me.

While Dizzy didn't want to make a fuss about the Savoy in Argentina, he did make one when we were in São Paulo, Brazil, our last stop on the tour after a short gig in Uruguay. We were asked to visit Casa Roosevelt (the Franklin D. Roosevelt School), a U.S.-sponsored school where the children were taught English. Dizzy talked with the kids, answered questions and received a tremendous reception. When he invited them to his next performance, the children told him they could not afford the tickets. Dizzy was aghast that these kids in their early teens would be required to buy tickets.

Dizzy didn't hesitate. He told the children (and indirectly ANTA), "If you can't come in free, I'm not playing." The word got out, and ANTA revised its policy as it pertained to this event. The kids came and, most importantly, they didn't have to pay. I had read that Dizzy took the same position on his tour of the Middle East, stating in Karachi, Pakistan and Ankara, Turkey that he wouldn't play if children, who could not afford tickets, weren't admitted.

Most people never saw this attribute in Dizzy because he was somewhat of a clown on stage. He was comedic, never letting his guard down. The incident at the Roosevelt school revealed his serious side. As his friend, I knew he had it, and I was glad he displayed his values publicly.

On a more pleasant note, Dizzy and I were having lunch in a hotel restaurant in Rio when we heard music, music that sounded damn good. It was obvious that the musicians were rehearsing. At almost the same moment, Dizzy and I, brothers of the heart and mind, had the identical idea. I went to get my recording equipment while he retrieved his trumpet from his hotel room.

We walked into the room where the musicians were rehearsing. They recognized Dizzy immediately and were stunned. It was like a deity had entered. They were awed, and reacted as if in the presence of a god. He joined the band, I set up my equipment, and we recorded about an hour of mostly bossa nova and samba music.

Brazil was the last stop and we flew home from Rio. Unfortunately, we had another major scare in the air as we did when our plane lost two engines on the route from Ecuador to Argentina. We encountered hurricane-force winds that tossed our four-propeller Lockheed around like a rowboat on the ocean in a storm.

Several of us, not wearing seat belts, hit the plane's ceiling. I was among them, and when I dropped down between the seats, I hurt my tailbone. Obviously, we were all scared and I saw Lorraine giving her prayer beads a special workout. However, we landed safely in the Dominican Republic where we refueled. The plane was inspected, and after officials were confident the plane hadn't suffered any damage, we continued the flight to the States.

The trip was considered a major diplomatic triumph. Dizzy was hailed for his music, as well as for his political skills, and the media, which usually tends to be cynical, praised the results of the tour.

I kept the tapes I recorded for about 45 years before deciding to go public with the music. I did ask Granz, the jazz impresario, to approve the release since Dizzy was under contract with him at the time of the 1956 tour. Granz was living in Switzerland, and in 1998 he signed papers that permitted me to produce the music. He died in 2001, the year the CDs were released.

In the liner notes for Volume 3, I thanked Granz, stating, "Thanks for the memories of all the great recordings you produced, and thanks for helping to make this happen."

I also expressed my gratitude to Jacques Muyal, a jazz aficionado who lived near Granz in Switzerland and who went to see Granz to obtain his signature. I said in the notes, "Thanks for being the messenger and dear friend. This is also from the man we all loved — John Birks Gillespie." And I signed it, "Later, Dave and Lorraine."

I worked with about 13 hours of tape and I produced three volumes of CDs entitled "Dizzy in South America." Unfortunately, I released this music after Dizzy died in 1993, and I regret that very much. Someday, I hope to produce CDs from the rest of the tapes, about 10 hours, because I feel strongly that the public should have the opportunity to hear the music from this history-making tour.

The music was produced under Red Anchor Productions (RAP), a company I founded. Again, I used the red anchor as a logo, the same logo I used for Marine Services Corp. and Marine Pollution Control. The CDs were released through Consolidated Artists Productions, Inc., which was founded by jazz pianist Mike Longo, who had worked with Dizzy for about 24 years and was among his closest friends.

Two CDs of Volume 3 contain interviews I conducted about a year before their release with participants in the 1956 tour in which they reminisce about the experience. I interviewed: Quincy Jones, Phil Woods, Billy Mitchell, Charlie Persip, Benny Golson, Rod Levitt, Lalo Schifrin, and Dizzy's cousin, Marion "Boo" Frazier, who managed the logistics on the trip. Including the interviews, the three volumes total a little over three hours. Incidentally, in one interview, several of the musicians discuss the harrowing flight through the vicious, life-threatening hurricane from Brazil to the U.S. There is much laughter on the CD in recalling the flight, although, at the time, we did not believe the situation was very funny.

The interviews also include one with Dizzy that I recorded when we were in Brazil. In it, Dizzy articulates his philosophy about jazz, a lesson I never forgot. He said jazz can be played on _any_ instrument; jazz is a matter of rhythm, and its effectiveness rests on the individual interpreting the music.

The CDs include some of Dizzy's classics, such as: "Manteca," "A Night in Tunisia," "Begin the Beguine," "Tin Tin Deo," "School Days," as well as the music recorded in Osvaldo Fresedo's club in Argentina, and the impromptu bossa nova and samba session in Brazil.

Despite the ugliness of the Savoy incident, I believe the tour was a phenomenal achievement. It demonstrated that despite the racial tensions in the U.S. at the time, Americans were committed to human and equal rights.

Fifty years later, in October 2006, the University of Southern California held a celebration to mark the historic tour, and I was flattered and privileged to be honored at this ceremony for my work in recording the music, and producing the CDs. The event was entitled "Jazz, Public Diplomacy and Dizzy Gillespie."

Regrettably, some of the members of the band had passed away. Among those attending were Quincy Jones, Lalo Schifrin, and James Moody. Also attending was Adam Clayton Powell III, the son of the Harlem congressman who was instrumental in pressuring President Eisenhower to initiate U.S-sponsored tours of jazz music to different countries.

I think that former Secretary of State Condoleezza Rice captured the meaning of the tour and Dizzy's impact when she said in a satellite message to the conference, "The music of Dizzy Gillespie spoke the language of freedom to think; to innovate; and to speak in one's own voice."

Moreover, people in four countries had an opportunity to hear one of the greatest trumpet players ever to blow the horn as well as his band members who were world-class artists themselves.

For me, it was a special privilege to record the music for posterity, and witness on the world stage once more, the exceptional talents of my brother, a man who made immeasurable contributions to the development of various jazz forms but, also, with his genius, influenced the interpretation of all kinds of music forever.

ARGO RECORDS

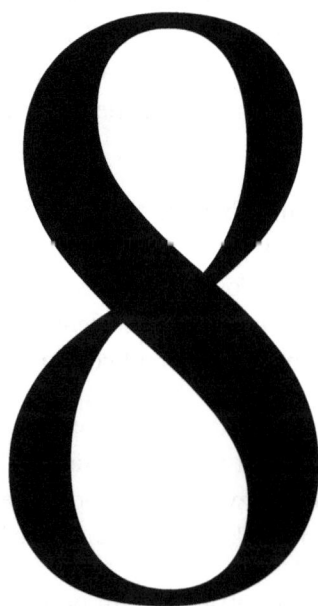

—●—

The trip to South America was an exhilarating experience. Throughout the tour, I listened to some of the best jazz music in the world and I was part of an entourage that was comprised of the most talented artists on the planet. It may be a cliché, yet it was true nevertheless: I had an once-in-a-lifetime experience.

Most important, in sponsoring this tour, the U.S. sent an important message in South America and indirectly to the world: America was committed to an integrated society. True, in 1956, race relations were still raw and very divisive in this country. The Civil Rights Movement was in its embryonic stage. Martin Luther King, Jr. was just beginning to make headlines. Only a year later, in 1957, President Eisenhower federalized the Arkansas National Guard and sent 1,000 troops from the 101st Airborne Division to Little Rock, Arkansas, when the state's governor, Orval E. Faubus, defied orders to integrate Arkansas schools.

The implied message of our tour was that, while we had racial problems, we were committed to solving them. One might argue the trip was intended to send that message to the bigots at home, those fighting efforts to create a society based on equality for all. I felt like I was part of history, the history of jazz, and the history of this country.

And, of course, the camaraderie was indescribable. This was a fun-loving group, as jazz musicians are prone to be. Let me cover the issue of drug use and get it out of the way. Yes, a few were addicted to hard drugs, but I never saw Dizzy use them in my almost 50 years as his friend. I had read that he once became ill in New York at the Village Vanguard after ingesting heroin. I was not there and it may be true.

In writing about that incident, Donald L. Maggin states in his book, *The Life and Times of Dizzy Gillespie*, "This was the first and only time in his life that Dizzy had touched heroin, and his system couldn't take it." Maggin reports that Dizzy was deceived when the dealer, who sold him the drugs, told Dizzy it was cocaine.

Dizzy's use of stimulants was restricted to alcohol and tobacco. Did he smoke marijuana? Yes, he did; we all did. The fact is marijuana was legal until the mid-1930s. We all smoked and enjoyed the so-called joints. As he got older, Dizzy made a point of cutting down on alcohol and tobacco of all kinds.

So returning home from South America was like coming off a high. This seems to be an appropriate description after my discussion of the use of pot in the previous paragraph. It was a letdown; an extreme letdown.

I returned to my father's business, and resumed my responsibilities as a yardman and oil sample tester which involved testing how much water and sediment was in oil. I drove trucks, worked in the yard, picked up oil to be recycled, spread oil on gravel roads, and carried out a variety of other duties.

My relationship with Dizzy was again similar to the one I had with him before the tour. Basically, we kept in touch by phone, and I visited him at gigs throughout the country. I regretted not being more involved with him, but my commitment to jazz did not diminish. Slowly, by chance, I was led to take a full-time job in jazz, my first, with the Chicago-based company, Chess Records, which specialized in blues, R&B, soul and gospel.

My evolvement to full-time employment started when Bess Bonnier, a very talented blind jazz pianist from Grosse Pointe, Michigan, a suburb southeast of Detroit, asked if I could put her in touch with the right people to help her career. She asked me about going on the road. I gave her a list of people to contact, which she did, including a very powerful and connected booking agent in Chicago, Fred Williamson, a vice president at the Associated Booking Corporation. I also sent her to Phil and Leonard Chess, Polish immigrants who had founded Chess Records.

Author Nadine Cohodas's book, *Spinning Blues Into Gold: The Chess Brothers and the Legendary Chess Records*, tells the story of how these two started the company and promoted such blues icons as McKinley Morganfield, an "immigrant" from a Mississippi cotton plantation and better known as Muddy Waters, Howlin' Wolf (Chester Arthur Burnett), Chuck Berry, Etta James and Bo Diddley (Ellas Otha Bates.)

During Bonnier's visit to Chess, I received a phone call from Phil and Leonard Chess, who had me on the speaker phone with Bonnier present. They asked, "Hey, Dave, this broad any good?" Of course, it was an uncomfortable situation. I told them I wouldn't have sent her if I didn't think she was talented.

"So Dave, if you think so much of her, why don't you come in and record her?"

They launched Argo Records, a division of Chess, as a jazz label with the help of Jack Tracy, editor of the jazz magazine *DownBeat* in the mid-1950s. I produced a record with Bonnier called "The Theme for the Tall One," which is still considered a collector's item by many jazz buffs. It was my first job for Argo, as it was for Bonnier. She ended up having a very successful career. She died at 83 in 2011.

The Chess brothers hired me on a project basis as an A&R man to produce recordings. They told me that anytime I had an idea for a recording, they would pay me while I was "away from the old man," and to "come in and do your thing."

I worked on individual projects for Chess for about six months before they hired me as a full-time employee to head the creative department in 1958. I was the proverbial man who came to dinner and stayed. Argo's motto was "Audio Odyssey by Argo," and I would undertake a two-year odyssey with the company.

I was commuting to Chicago from Detroit, which was very expensive, and when I asked for more money, I can still remember Leonard Chess responding, "What are you? One of my relatives?" They paid me $200 a week, but it cost me $25 (one way) to fly to Chicago. I was not making a lot of money. The message was clear. Since I wasn't a relative, I should not expect a raise. That is not to say I would have received one if I had been *mishpacha* (a relative.) They were tough guys.

While Chess covered some of my expenses, to save money, when I stayed in Chicago during the week, I would sleep on a couch in Chess's offices. My "roommate" was Boo Frazier, Dizzy's cousin, who was on the 1956 trip to South America and whom I interviewed on the CDs I released of that trip. Frazier had been a DJ in the South, and recognizing that Frazier's career was at a dead end, Dizzy asked me if I could find Frazier a job. I approached the Chess brothers, and they hired Frazier to package records.

Dizzy was very grateful, and Frazier ultimately became a promoter, working for many jazz musicians, including jazz trumpeter Herb Alpert (of Herb Alpert's Tijuana Brass), and Frazier enjoyed a very fruitful career.

Frazier slept in the office as well, on an Army cot, and, to be fair, I would trade places with him periodically. I put up with sleeping on a couch, and every other week on an Army cot, cleaning up in an adjacent bathroom, and barely making it financially because of the love I had for what I was doing. And, I might add, Frazier had the same love for the music.

Another of my major recordings at Argo was with Ahmad Jamal, an outstanding jazz pianist. He had approached me at the recommendation of Howard McGhee, a jazz trumpeter, when I launched the Emanon label in 1948. I was still living with my parents, and all we had was an upright piano. To get the best sound during the audition, I took him to the home of my brother, Morris, who had a grand piano. Jamal was superb. Unfortunately, I had to tell him I didn't have the resources to do anything for him. Both of us, at the time, were highly disappointed.

When I joined to run Argo, Jamal was already under contract with the Chess brothers which gave me the opportunity to work with him. I put together an album, "At the Pershing: But Not for Me," which he had recorded at a live performance with his trio in the Pershing Lounge of Chicago's Pershing Hotel. It was very well received by jazz fans. I also edited his classic, "Poinciana," which was also recorded at the Pershing Lounge. Jamal was accompanied by bassist Israel Crosby and drummer Vernell Fournier, and the piece was used as the sound track for the movie, "The Bridges of Madison County," which was directed by Clint Eastwood. I didn't know the music was in the film until I went to see the movie. It required editing because it was too long to be played on the radio or in jukeboxes. We cut it down from eight minutes and 45 seconds to two minutes and 40 seconds. I also did four other albums with Jamal called, "Jamal at the Penthouse," "Portfolio of Ahmad Jamal," "Ahmad Jamal Trio: Complete Live at the Spotlite Club," and "Extensions."

Then I produced pieces with jazz pianist Ramsey Lewis which included a jazz version of the opera "Carmen" in an album called "Ramsey Lewis Trio – Carmen." We also did an album called "Lem Winchester and the Ramsey Lewis Trio." The album was a tribute to Clifford "Brownie" Brown, a highly talented trumpet player from Wilmington, Delaware who was killed in a car accident on the Pennsylvania Turnpike while traveling from one gig to another in 1956. He was only 25. The two other musicians making up the Ramsey Lewis Trio were El Dee Young, bass, and Red Holt, drums.

Two of the songs on the album, "Joy Spring" and "Sandu," were composed by Brown. Another piece included was a "Message from Boysie" by Robert Lowery, a jazz music teacher nicknamed "Boysie" who taught Brown, as well as many other musicians, including trumpeter Marcus Belgrave, who became world famous. Like Brown, Lowery was also from Wilmington, Delaware, as was Lem.

Brown was a close friend of Lem Winchester who also died too young. Lem was an exceptional artist, principally playing the vibraphone. He also played several other instruments, including the flute, piccolo, and baritone horn, and tried his hand at tenor sax, mellophone, and clarinet. A nine-year veteran policeman in Wilmington, Lem was assigned to a black neighborhood where he was loved, especially by the kids. One of his trademarks was to fold a two dollar bill into a ring and when any of the kids graduated from high school, he would slip it on their fingers. I don't know how many of those he gave away but, given the number of kids involved over the years, it had to amount to a lot of money, especially for a cop who didn't earn much.

He gave rings to my kids who called him "Uncle Lem" when he stayed at my house. I still have one of those rings. He even went to my kids' bedroom and read them stories, using a Donald Duck voice to imitate the characters in the book. That showed the depth of the man, the kind of man he was.

Lem and I became very close friends, and he asked my advice on whether he should continue his career as a cop or try his hand at making a living as a full-time jazz musician. I recognized his enormous talent and suggested that he give jazz a try, which he did. He was becoming quite famous in the jazz world when, one day, in January 1961, his wife, Sis, called me at about 1 a.m. with the kind of news everyone dreads receiving.

Sis told me that Lem was playing at the Topper Club and Lounge in Indianapolis, Indiana. During a break, he was sitting at the bar and noticed a revolver on a shelf. He asked to see it and told the bartender he would demonstrate a trick playing Russian roulette. Apparently, he had done this trick many times, except he was not familiar with the revolver he was handed.

Jet Magazine reported on February 2, 1961: [...Winchester] mistook a Smith & Wesson for a .38 caliber Colt "police special" in the Russian roulette demonstration. Police explained that because the Colt's cylinder revolved counter-clockwise, the chances are 1,000-1 that the hammer will not fall on a live chamber once a shell is removed. A Smith & Wesson revolves clockwise, reducing the odds to five-to-one, they said."*

When Lem pulled the trigger with the gun at his head, it went off, killing him instantly. He was only 32, and left his wife with three young sons. I was devastated, crushed by the news, as were his many other friends and countless fans. Lem was a man with a heart, and I still remember that when I left Argo in 1960, he asked, "Do you need any money? I love you and if you

---

*That report was not accurate. In doing research on the incident, we talked to Sergeant Scot Sowden, of the Wilmington Delaware Police Department, who said the issue had nothing to do with odds since both revolvers had six cylinders. He explained that if you put a bullet in the 11 o'clock position on a Smith & Wesson revolver, when you pull the trigger, the cylinder will rotate counter-clockwise (to the left), away from the hammer which fires the bullet. On a Colt, the cylinder rotates clockwise. Thus, when Lem, mistaking a Colt for a Smith & Wesson revolver, inserted the bullet at 11 o'clock, the cylinder rotated clockwise (to the right) and it fired.

need any help, I'm here to help you." I lost a close friend, one that I still miss very much, and the jazz world lost an irreplaceable talent.

I had another very sad experience with an extraordinarily talented jazz musician, James Moody. That one, I was thrilled, ultimately turned out well. I had known Moody, who played tenor and alto sax as well as the flute, for more than 14 years. He had played with Dizzy off and on for three years, but he had very serious problems with alcohol. Argo had him under contract, and I was told that Moody "wasn't well" and had voluntarily committed himself to the Overbrook Sanitarium in Cedar Grove, New Jersey, which treated patients with addictions and mental illnesses. The irony was that Overbrook sat on a cliff just above the Meadowbrook Country Club, a music mecca. Its owner, Frank Dailey, booked some of the country's most famous big bands, as well as such singing stars as Frank Sinatra.

Moody owed Argo several albums, but was not in the condition to do them. I was saddened that such an outstanding artist was losing his fight against alcohol addiction when Moody, after five months at Overbrook, called me to say he was clean. The Chess brothers suggested I visit him to make an assessment whether Moody was ready to play. My friend, J.C. Heard, the jazz drummer, and I visited Moody. The entire atmosphere depressed me. It was like a jail with bars on the windows and mentally ill patients walking around or sitting, somewhat dazed, almost everywhere. Some were talking to themselves, some were in restraints. It was like a scene out of the movies.

We met Moody in what they called the "day room" of Ward 33. It was clear to me, he was not in good shape. But his spirit, his musical spirit, was alive. He wanted to play again and soon, telling me that he had written some music, including one piece on the institution that he had entitled, "Last Train from Overbrook." He had a rolled up manuscript in his hands which he clutched to his chest just like Lalo Schifrin had done when I met him in the hall of our hotel in Buenos Aires, Argentina.

I talked to his doctors and they thought playing would be good for Moody. It was evident they were prepared to release him. The medical personnel knew about Moody and what a talent he was. They were very sympathetic. We decided to give Moody a shot and record him. We made arrangements for Moody to travel to Chicago *by train*, which made his composition so symbolic. And he was to travel by himself. I sent him tickets and Moody understood that, in letting him travel alone, we were expressing trust in him, that we had confidence that he would stay "straight."

I had a scheduling conflict because I was to record Ahmad Jamal at the Spotlite Club in Washington, D.C. just when Moody was on his way to Chicago. While we traveled separately, our mutual "strength and trust" in each other promised that this venture would not fail. Both of us knew that this would be a challenge. We did not articulate it but the message was clear: "We're gonna make it, baby." And Moody came through; he met the challenge, which could not have been easy for him.

Moody did not have any instruments, so I called the Selmer Instrument Company, a famous musical instrument manufacturer, and asked if the company would donate a couple of saxes and a flute. When I told the company's representatives that I was making the request for Moody, they responded, "No problem, just tell us what you need." Two saxes and a flute were in Chicago waiting for us when Moody and I arrived on Labor Day in 1958 from New Jersey and D.C., respectively.

We had an 18-piece orchestra and the leader was Johnny Pate, who was becoming a jazz star. The session was a highly emotional experience because everyone understood the underlying meaning of the "Last Train from Overbrook." To our surprise, Moody wasn't rusty at all. He played with feeling and emotion as he always did.

As we were recording Moody on his flute, he hit a bad note and said, instinctively, in time with the music, "Better do it again…I goofed…yes…I goofed…on the record." There were some chuckles, followed by a few seconds of silence as the musicians stopped playing. I announced immediately from the control room, "This is going to be on the LP." So we have a 45-second piece on the record called "The Moody One," which is labeled "false start" on the cover. To me this was a gem, showing that even the most talented of jazz artists were not infallible. Even the best make mistakes, but they move ahead nevertheless. Then Moody plays the entire piece correctly, and it runs two minutes and 38 seconds.

I kept a similar remark on a recording I made with Dizzy on the 1956 South American trip when, while introducing a tune, he recognized how serious he was becoming, and suddenly remarked, "I'm out of character..."

Dizzy, always a comic on stage, someone who wanted to make people laugh as well as enjoy his music, felt he had become too formal in addressing the audience. As he was speaking, he realized that he was not in character, at least not for Dizzy Gillespie. He blurted out his amazement on how he unknowingly abandoned the light-hearted role he always had on stage. He actually turned away from the microphone when he said it, but we captured his remark on our sound equipment. I was not going to have anyone talk me out of using it on the CD. It was, in a word, precious and revealing, making this exceptional trumpet player, whom many considered a "jazz god," human.

The Moody album turned out beautifully, and for the cover design we hired Vytas Valaitis, a famous photographer, who did many shoots for *Newsweek Magazine*. I don't know technically how he achieved the dramatic effect of the train featured on the cover. I do know he used three separate negatives and blended them together. The train, with what appears to be lightning hitting it, certainly is symbolic of the road Moody had to travel musically, psychologically, and emotionally, to win the battle over his addiction.

The album did very well, and Moody enjoyed a very rewarding career, staying "straight" while traveling the world. He had entitled his piece appropriately. He never again had to take a train or any other kind of transportation from an institution that treated alcoholics. He passed away in 2010.

I produced two albums at Argo that I recorded in one night. The albums were with jazz pianist Barry Harris and saxophonist Sonny Stitt, both of whom ultimately enjoyed international fame. With Harris, I produced a record called "Breakin' It Up." To illustrate the cover, I had Barry stand in the fire door of a theater that had been demolished on the east side of Detroit. That doorway was all that was left of the theater, and it made perfect sense to use it for the album's cover. Joining Harris were William Austin, bass, and Frank Gant, drums.

Stitt's album, "Burnin'," created a potential legal problem. When he signed with another label, he still was responsible for recording one more album for Chess. He met his obligation but we could not actively promote it. Rather than write liner notes for the album, I simply put Stitt's photo on both the front and back covers of the record. Problem solved, and the record still made its mark in the jazz market even without the notes.

Two other albums, of which I was very proud, were "Shaw Nuff" with trumpeter Red Rodney, and one with the fantastic drummer, J.C. Heard, called "This is Me, J.C. Heard." Heard had played with the most successful bands in the history of jazz, including Count Basie, Duke Ellington, Benny Goodman and others. When he started his own orchestra, he featured a then-very-young and unknown singer, Sarah Vaughan.

I was enjoying the work at Chess when my brother, Morris, called to tell me our father was very ill and asked me to rejoin the family business. I was torn and, after some anguished debate with myself, I resigned from Chess in February 1960, and returned to Detroit to work again in all the facets of the oil refining business. My father died four months after I rejoined the family business.

Before I left Argo, I recorded one last album called "An Hour with Ramsey Lewis," which featured Lewis, piano; El Dee Young, bass; and Red Holt, drums. When we finished, we hugged, and there were a few tears. They knew I was leaving.

The best compliment I received for my two years at Chess came when Ramsey Lewis told me that Leonard Chess, a very tough guy not given to sentimentality, admitted that the biggest mistake he had made in the business was to let me go. I did not get any raises at Chess since I was not a relative, but I received a compliment, admittedly indirectly, for which I was very grateful.

I never worked for anyone else in the jazz business again. That did not mean I gave up my interests in jazz or that I was "breakin' it up" with Dizzy.

No way.

FREELANCE A&R MAN; DIZZY RUNS FOR PRESIDENT

9

—❦—

Jazz was in my blood. It was part of my DNA. I would not and could not let go.

While on a business path to create Marine Pollution Control, in jazz, for the next 40 years, I had a parallel career as a freelance A&R man, and I was very proud to be one. Musicians would call me to assist them, or I would call artists if I had ideas for an album.

As I have indicated, the role of an A&R man is a sensitive one. He is the director of the respective project while serving also as a counselor, psychiatrist, friend, confidant, negotiator, and compromiser. He juggles all these responsibilities to create the proper atmosphere in which to produce the best music, music that makes the participants proud and moves listeners. He has to establish warmth in the recording studio that brings out the best in the artists.

It is not an easy job, and I was extremely flattered and proud that these world-class talents put their trust, confidence and faith in me: a man who did not play an instrument, could not read music, and had no formal training whatsoever in music.

The first project I undertook after leaving Argo was to produce a jazz festival in Birmingham, Michigan, a primarily white suburb north of Detroit.

Bob Maxwell, a well-known Detroit DJ with whom, as I have mentioned, I crossed paths many times in my jazz endeavors, came up with the idea in discussions with Dr. Richard Galpin, a pediatrician, who was a jazz buff. Maxwell, a Birmingham resident, introduced me to the city's decision-makers who included executives at the local paper, the *Birmingham Eccentric*, leaders of the city's cultural and civic organizations, and Birmingham's elected officials. After a few meetings, they hired me to organize the festival.

The festival was held in the Geodesic Dome in Shain Park in 1960. The artists who participated were: Nick Fiore, bass; J.C. Heard, Dick Riordan, drums; Junior Mance, Bess Bonnier, Johnny Griffin, piano; Sandy Mosse, tenor sax; Joe Kennedy, violin; Baron "Toots" Thielemans, harmonica and guitar; Lem Winchester, vibes; and Johnny Griffith, tenor saxophone and leader of the Johnny Griffith Trio.

Given the extremely favorable response in the Detroit area, I was asked to produce a second one the following year. Again, I brought in the best talent from throughout the country, and the musicians included: Wynton Kelly, piano; Nick Fiore, bass; J.C. Heard, drums; Sandy Mosse, Oliver Nelson, Billy Mitchell, tenor sax; Jimmy Wilkins and his 16-piece Big Band; Al Grey, trombone; Joe Newman, trumpet; Clark Terry, trumpet and flugelhorn; Les Spann, guitar; and Joe Carroll, vocalist.

I recorded the music at both festivals, and 40 years later (2001-2002) I released five CDs of the 1960 and 1961 concerts under the Red Anchor Productions label. I dedicated the 1961 CDs to Lem Winchester. (He died in the gun accident before the second jazz festival was held.) In the liner notes I wrote: "Lem, we will never forget your greatness as a human being, and above all, just plain you. Straight ahead — Dave Usher."

After the first concert I spoke briefly to the audience, stating I hoped that "We could enjoy many more years of stuff like this," and Birmingham did just that. The festival was an annual event in Birmingham for almost 50 years. It ended in 2008 when, due to depressed economic conditions, the city wasn't able to obtain the necessary supporting sponsorships.

For my next freelancing project I produced an album with violinist Joe Kennedy, who was a close friend of Ahmad Jamal. An extraordinary talent, the liner notes stated, "He is not the President's father [Joe Kennedy, father of John F. Kennedy], but one of the presidents of the modern violin." I was introduced to Kennedy by Jamal, who had grown up with Kennedy when they both lived in Pittsburgh.

The album was called "Strings by Candlelight" and it was an example of how my two careers on rare occasions overlapped. I was working on a ship, the *SS Expeditor* of American Export Lines, and the captain, Charlie Walther, and I became very close friends. He called me "Moish" and when Walther learned that I had a recording date with Kennedy in New York at the same time I was supposed to be working on his ship, he told me, "Moish, you go and record and don't worry about a thing. I'll supervise your crew and make sure it does everything you want it to do."

Then he added, "At 2 p.m. when you're recording in New York, I'll be under the Mackinac Bridge [which connects the Upper and Lower Michigan peninsulas], and I'll give a blast that they'll never forget." This was coming from a man I was supposed to be working for. That's how close we were.

The cover of the album is another story. After completing the recording, I returned to the ship a few weeks later, and Walther was enthralled by the music. He was sitting by a candle in the captain's salon with a shipping agent from Cleveland, Nicki Koebetis. I asked Walther to light a cigarette, and then I covered the agent's face on the camera lens with a see-through cleaning tissue which gave the photo a mystical quality. It's a very romantic photo and that's why we called the album, "Strings by Candlelight."

Another album I did with Kennedy was called "Accentuate the Positive," and it featured Baron "Toots" Thielemans, who played the harmonica and the guitar. He was considered, arguably, the best harmonica player of the 20th Century.

Meanwhile, my relationship with Dizzy consisted of staying in touch with him by telephone, flying to his gigs, and periodic travel to Europe, South America and Africa.

Then, one day in 1964, while I was talking to him by phone, he nonchalantly told me he was running for president. He would run as an independent write-in candidate against the Democratic incumbent, Lyndon B. Johnson, and the Republican challenger, Senator Barry Goldwater, of Arizona.

"That's nice," I responded not knowing any of the background or, frankly, what he was talking about. After some research, I learned that in the 1940s and '50s, "Dizzy Gillespie for President" buttons were manufactured by Dizzy's booking agency, the Associated Booking Corporation. At the time, no one paid any attention to them.

The gag turned serious in the early '60s, and it happened by chance. The woman who was to become Dizzy's Southern California campaign manager, Patricia Willard, of Washington, D.C., reminiscing about the campaign to elect Dizzy president, wrote in a December 2012 article in *DownBeat*, that an old "Dizzy Gillespie for President" button showed up in the mailbox of syndicated columnist and former *DownBeat* editor, Ralph J. Gleason, who ran with the idea. Gleason's wife, Jeannie, became Dizzy's campaign manager and his chief advisor.

The bebop vocalist Jon Hendricks wrote words for a campaign song and its lyrics were sung to the tune of "Salt Peanuts" which Dizzy wrote. The lyrics were:

Intro: *Vote Diz, Vote Diz, Vote Diz*
          Vote for Diz, Vote for Diz
          He'll show you where it is
          Vote Dizzy! Vote Dizzy!

Chorus: *You want a good President who's willing to run*
          Vote Dizzy! Vote Dizzy!
          You wanna make government a barrel of fun
          Vote Dizzy! Vote Dizzy!
          Your politics oughta be a groovier thing
          Vote Dizzy! Vote Dizzy!
          So get a good President who's willing to swing
          Vote Dizzy! Vote Dizzy!

Bridge: *Show the Republic where it is*
                Give them a Democratic Diz, really he is

Last Eight: *Your political leaders spout a lot of hot air*
                Vote Dizzy! Vote Dizzy!
                But Dizzy blows trumpet so you really don't care
                Vote Dizzy! Vote Dizzy!

Interlude: *You oughta spend your money in a groovier way*
                —Every cent
                Get that badge of the People's only candidate
                Dizzy for President

The John Birks Society, a play on the name of the John Birch Society, the extreme right-wing reactionary organization, was organized to promote the campaign which, at one point, had chapters in 25 states. The write-in campaign for president was launched at a rally in Chicago. Asked why he was running for president, Dizzy responded, "Because we need one." He added, humorously, "I am no dark horse candidate."

Almost everyone agreed the campaign was somewhat of a gag. Yet, it did have a serious tone in that Dizzy was able to talk about political issues that were important to him. Before his "run," for president, he seldom used the stage for politics, but now he could and would have his say. Dizzy said in his 1980 autobiography when he announced his candidacy, "It wasn't just a publicity stunt." At one press conference, Willard wrote in *DownBeat*, that a radio reporter from CBS/KNX stomped out angrily, shouting, "I thought this would be lots of laughs. But this guy's serious."

Willard reported in her article:

> "Miriam Makeba, jazz singer and Civil Rights activist, appeared at a rally in Palo Alto, California. Clint Eastwood (actor) requested a bumper sticker, U.S. Rep. Barbara Jordan, of Texas, wore her Dizzy button on the floor of the House."

Dizzy chose as his running mate, Ramona Crowell, whom he had met, along with her husband, Kenney, when she approached him in a jazz club to ask permission to use his likeness on sweatshirts long before the 1964 campaign. In 2012, Berl interviewed Crowell by telephone at her home in Berkeley, California. She was 86 at the time.

She told Berl she had never been involved in politics and agreed to join the ticket as a vice presidential candidate because "It would be fun, and it was." She was a member of the Assiniboine Tribe of the Sioux Nation, but she said Dizzy did not choose her because of her ethnic background. She said he chose her because they were friends, and probably because she had a hand in starting what began as a "lighthearted" idea. She accepted the "nomination" readily, stating she was "flattered," asking, "Wouldn't you be?"

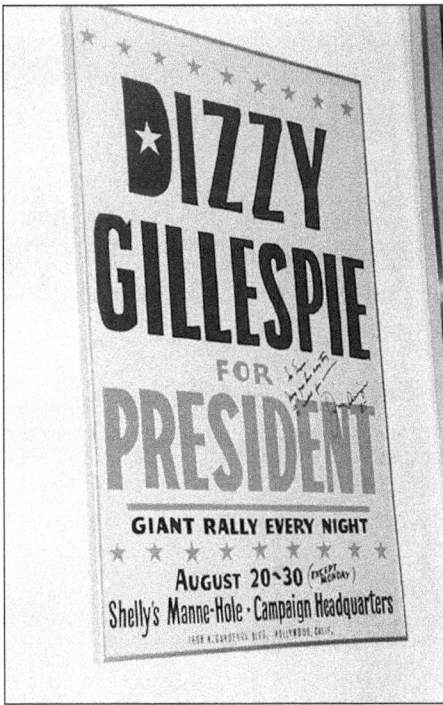

Poster promotiong "Dizzy Gillespie for President" in 1964.

She said she and Dizzy never discussed issues or policies, nor did she participate in choosing the somewhat "unique" cabinet that Dizzy said he would appoint, if elected. "Dizzy did all that," she said although she added that she did some campaigning in jazz clubs and music venues.

If elected, Dizzy said he would end the Vietnam War which was just beginning at the time, give full diplomatic recognition to China, and health care and education would be free. Other policies involved abolishing the income tax, and replacing it by legalizing the numbers game which would be run by the government. "We'd make more money," he said.

A pacifist, Dizzy also promised to abolish the Departments of the Army and Navy. As to President Kennedy's challenge to send a man to the moon, he said he would make sure a black man would be considered for the historic flight. If they couldn't find a qualified candidate, he would volunteer to go.

In the workplace, he said those applying for jobs would wear hoods so prospective employers would not know the race of candidates until they were hired.

He promised that, if elected, he would call the White House the "Blues House," and use the word "ministry" instead of "secretary" for cabinet positions because it gave the position more dignity. The candidates for his cabinet would be composed primarily of jazz legends. Here is a list of some of the artists he said he would appoint:

Band Leader Duke Ellington, minister of state. Some "informed sources" reported that Dizzy also considered boxing champion, Muhammad "The Greatest" Ali, for this position, as well as Bo Diddley, vocalist, guitarist, and songwriter.

Trumpeter Miles Davis, director of the CIA.

Drummer Max Roach, minister of defense.

Bassist Charles Mingus, minister of peace ("Because he'll take a piece of your head faster than anyone I know.")

Pianist, soul singer Ray Charles, librarian of Congress.

Trumpeter Louis "Satchmo" Armstrong, minister of agriculture.

Pianist Mary Lou Williams, who had a religious bent, ambassador to the Vatican.

Pianist Thelonious Monk, roving plenipotentiary (ambassador.)

Minister and human rights activist, Malcolm X, attorney general, "because it would be good to have him on our side for a change."

Vocalist Jon Hendricks, poet laureate.

Saxophonist Benny Carter, minister to the United Nations.

Jazz vocalist Peggy Lee, ministress of labor.

Jeannie Gleason, Dizzy's campaign manager, ministress of the treasury.

He proposed appointing Mississippi Governor Ross Barnett, a staunch segregationist, U.S. Information Agency director in the Congo, and targeted Alabama Governor George Wallace, also an ardent segregationist, for deportation to Vietnam.

In her *DownBeat* article, Willard wrote:

> "I suggested that we should anticipate our candidate's victory with a *DownBeat* cover photo of him taking the oath of office in front of the Manne-Hole [a jazz club in Hollywood named for Shelly Manne, drummer.} *DownBeat* Associate Editor John A. Tynan loved the idea but said there was no budget for such a set-up.

> "Shelly Manne, feeling enthusiastic about the coup of having his club on the cover of *DownBeat*, agreed to underwrite expenses. Shelly hired carpenters to erect a speaker's platform sturdy enough for six men and a large U.S. flag.

> "President Gillespie and his Supreme Court justices (Kenny Barron, piano; James Moody, sax; Chris White, bass; Rudy Collins, drums; and Shelly) were outfitted at Western Costume Company. I donned my Dizzy sweatshirt, and I assembled my children, their friends, Tynan, and a bunch of dedicated friends of the musicians. Until now, most people have never known that President Dizzy Gillespie's inauguration took place at Shelly's Manne-Hole in Hollywood. And nobody knew it was actually financed by Shelly Manne himself.

> "So what happened to the movement? Apparently, several hundred write-in votes for Dizzy were tabulated in 25 states, all of which had been circulating petitions to get his name placed on the 1964 ballot. The *National Observer* suggested that 1964 was an encouraging preparation for a more intense 1968 campaign. Dizzy was amenable

until his spiritual advisor counseled that running for political office was an ego trip, and against the principles of his Bahá'i Faith."

Dizzy received some write-in votes in 1964, but he obviously posed no serious challenge to the two major candidates. The proceeds Dizzy's campaign raised from the sale of buttons and other paraphernalia went to such organizations as the Congress for Racial Equality (CORE), and Dr. Martin Luther King Jr.'s Southern Christian Leadership Conference (SCLC.)

When the campaign ended, Dizzy said, "I liked the idea of running for president. And it would've been fun to be elected. I'd have fought for a disarmament program, and the establishment of a world government."

Dizzy maintained that his candidacy wasn't entirely a joke, stating that, "Anybody woulda made a better president than the ones we had in those times, dilly-dallying about protecting blacks in their civil and human rights, and carrying on secret wars against people around the world. I didn't think I had any choice. I had a real reason for running because the proceeds from the sale of buttons went to CORE and SCLC...and I could threaten the Democrats with a loss of votes and swing them to a more reasonable position on civil rights."

I don't know if Dizzy considered a presidential run in 1968, and his former running mate, Ramona Crowell, told us she did not know either. Dizzy does not mention 1968 in his autobiography and nor do any of the biographies. Dizzy flirted with another candidacy in 1972 when the incumbent Republican President Richard Nixon ran against Democratic Senator George McGovern, of South Dakota. However, Dizzy withdrew quickly, stating, as Willard reported, that participation in politics ran counter to the principles of the Bahá'i Faith, a religion to which he converted on April 4, 1968, the day Dr. Martin Luther King, Jr. was assassinated.

(In Cheraw, South Carolina, while the Gillespies were members of the United Methodist Church, Dizzy also attended the services at the town's Sanctified Church because he loved its raucous, soul-searing prayer music.)

My role in the campaign was restricted to wearing a "Dizzy Gillespie for President" button. I never was involved, nor did I discuss it with him at any length. I was too busy at Marine Services Corp., having returned to the family business only four years earlier. Most of the information here came from conversations I had at the time with people around him, Dizzy's autobiography, biographies on Dizzy, and from news reports. Dizzy did receive extensive publicity on his foray into politics from the media throughout the country.

Although I don't think anyone on his campaign staff really expected him to win, the write-in effort permitted Dizzy, as he said, to try and influence the political conversation about issues such as the mistreatment of blacks and the Vietnam War, issues that were very important to him. Always the prankster on stage, Dizzy had a thoughtful and contemplative side to him that he hid from the public when he performed.

On the lighter side, I always envisioned all these artists walking around the White House with their instruments, jamming whenever they could. I could also see Dizzy, as president, telling representatives of countries that were adversaries and had been invited to the White House, "Before we begin this meeting, let my cabinet members create the right atmosphere." After playing a few foot-stomping pieces, I think negotiations to reach settlements on the most difficult issues in the world would have been much simpler.

As for me, I would have loved to have been an A&R man in the White House.

RACE

10

—●—

I was often asked how Dizzy and I, opposites in race, religion, and cultural background, created such a trusting bond, and if race ever caused tensions between the two of us.

Those questions were particularly prevalent early in our relationship because, at the time, people still had very deep prejudices. In effect, we became a symbol of how barriers of color, religion and cultural backgrounds can be broken.

To the first part, I always answered that our foundation rested on trust and respect. We had a compatibility, a rapport. There was nothing we didn't share with each other, whether the issues involved professional problems or personal ones. We shared everything, and even when we differed in our views, we respected one another.

As to racial tensions, the answer is never, never in 50 years was there ever the slightest hint of racial animosity. Dizzy did not have any animosity toward others either, and he certainly had a right to be angry, given what blacks experienced in this country.

After all, he was born in a town that had been involved heavily in the slave trade, and as a young boy, it was not unusual for him to be called "boy" or "niggah" in segregated Cheraw, population 3,500. He drank at "colored only" drinking fountains and used restrooms marked similarly.

Yet Dizzy, always combative, did not turn away from bigoted insults. He frequently had fights with white boys who would taunt him, understanding all too well that the consequences could be dire. He never backed down when faced with racism and bigotry. I remember when, in the 1950s, at a time the racial divide was still very wide in the U.S., we were docking my boat after a day on Lake St. Clair on the shoreline of Grosse Pointe, Michigan, an upscale Detroit suburb which barred blacks and Jews from buying homes in the city. The residents were staring at Dizzy, and the question was clear in their eyes: Why was a black man boating with a white man — and so close to their city? Dizzy noticed the stares, and yelled out, "Oh, my goodness. Look how sun-tanned I got today."

Another question I encountered was whether any of the black musicians resented my friendship/partnership with Dizzy. No one ever said anything to me. I never felt any friction. I would guess that a few may have objected to a white being involved with, principally, black musicians, but if they had such feelings, they kept their misgivings to themselves, if for no other reason than they understood the unbreakable bond Dizzy and I enjoyed. They would not have wanted to anger him.

In Cheraw, given his talents as a musician at an early age as well as a dancer, he was "accepted" by the white community which frequently invited him to "white only" events and asked him to dance. As he did, his "sponsors" would throw dimes and quarters in appreciation. He was also an accomplished diver and, at white-only swimming pools, was asked to perform his dives. He was again rewarded by whites who tossed into the pool, coins which Dizzy retrieved.

Of course, he, like all blacks, resented the treatment blacks had to endure, and how they were denied their heritage in the South. Years later in New York when he immersed himself in Afro-Cuban music, he observed, "The Africa I was denied in South Carolina, I found in East Harlem."

As he grew older and became a professional musician, race became less of an issue. I don't remember him ever playing to black-only audiences. They were always integrated. One exception, in the early '50s, was in Washington, D.C. when he played to blacks only at an 11 p.m. show on the cruise ship, *Bear Mountain*, on the Potomac River, and earlier in the evening to an exclusively white audience. I also recall that for the white performance, the police were armed only with nightsticks, but for the black audience they also carried revolvers.

Somewhat ironically, Dizzy and his band were staying at an all-black hotel from which I was barred. The owners were afraid that my presence might cause trouble. When Dizzy heard that I would need to find a different hotel, he played peacemaker, negotiated with the management, and I was permitted to stay. When we traveled to places where white and blacks were separated, and we were not permitted to eat together, we just didn't eat. At the beginning of Dizzy's career, his band members were all black; in later years, he integrated his bands. Race was not the issue; talent was. If they played his kind of thing, they were in.

Dizzy gave credit to Norman Granz, the founder in the mid-'40s of Jazz at the Philharmonic, which sponsored concerts, tours, and produced records, for hiring black musicians when others discriminated against them. Granz was an integrationist in the jazz world, and had white and black musicians play together. In a two-hour taped interview in 1989 with Nat Hentoff, the widely acclaimed jazz critic, Dizzy said Granz, who was white and Jewish, opened doors for black musicians, and paid them fairly. When Granz's black musicians traveled, he made sure they stayed in first-class hotels and ate at first-class restaurants, Dizzy said.

Once, Dizzy told Hentoff, when he was arrested with other black musicians in Houston, Texas, for shooting dice — the arrest was more about racism than illegal gambling — Granz, who was backstage at a gig during the raid, bailed them out. "He (Granz) was death on prejudice," Dizzy said. (The renowned Ella Fitzgerald, jazz vocalist, was among those arrested.)

As I wrote, Dizzy always included whites in his numerous bands. Race was secondary to talent. For instance, Phil Woods, the highly talented white alto sax player, told me the story of how he sat in a bar one night, feeling sorry for himself when Dizzy "kidnapped" him, taking him to Dizzy's apartment where he asked Woods, "What's your problem?"

Woods said he felt that as a white "Irish honky" without rhythm, he would never make it. Dizzy told him to quit "whining," "to grow up" and "get your act together." Never mentioning race, Dizzy told Woods he had the talent and to stop complaining. Reemphasizing his point, Dizzy told Woods, "Bird [Charlie Parker] gave it to everyone. Bird took the music to all races. If you can hear it, you can have it." Woods went on to a highly productive career, and always credited Dizzy with giving him the confidence he needed.

Dizzy did not engage in a public dialogue on race even during the Civil Rights Movement. Of course, he had the utmost respect for and supported Dr. Martin Luther King, Jr. and other leaders in their fight for equal rights.

As I have written, even when he and his band were refused rooms at the Savoy Hotel in Buenos Aires because they were black, Dizzy didn't speak out. On that occasion, he was a representative of the U.S. and may not have wanted to create an international incident. He generally avoided making statements on racial politics except when he ran for president. When, periodically, he expressed his views, he could be very sarcastic, caustic and funny.

These occurrences were usually prompted by a bigoted insult or racial slur. For instance, in 1973, he spoke out on race at Ronnie Scott's Jazz Club in London* and he didn't hold back on that occasion. Let's face it, Dizzy was unpredictable, and many observed that was one reason he was called "Dizzy."

After some remarks that were not recorded about the heritage of blacks in Africa "before we got to America," Dizzy said:

"We gonna whip on you what we created in America, the blues, honey…this is what come out of that…you see it's a long story about the blues and the gospel and the spiritual…you see whitey…whitey…didn't allow us to have our traditional instrument which was the drum…

---

*Dizzy and his band, all agreed, were "on fire" at the club and their contract was extended. Peter Bould, an associate of Ronnie Scott, with Dizzy's permission, recorded the remaining sessions of Dizzy's gig. This music was never made public. At this writing, my company, Red Anchor Productions, and Mike Longo's Consolidated Artists Productions, Inc., are working on producing CDs of this historic event.

"[Dizzy beats on drum]…because we can talk through that sucker…we can talk through it, we could talk with that… before we came to America…but people were afraid that you would say something that they didn't know what you was talking about…understand?

"Not only wouldn't they let you talk with the drums, they wouldn't let you talk your language with nobody else…you were not allowed to speak your ancient tongue…if they caught you, you know what they did?

"If they caught you speaking anything besides pidgin English…If they find two guys speaking the same language on the same plantation, they'd sell one of them right quick…can you imagine about 500 people on a plantation with no one knowing what the other one is talking about…but that was the idea…

"But we got them because we got the blues…good God Almighty…we got the blues and we got jazz too…jazz is an evolutionary process of the blues…"

Dizzy made his comments just before introducing a new piece called "The Truth" composed by Mike Longo, his pianist, which Dizzy called "a masterpiece." And he also commended Al Gafa, the guitarist. I believe he did this because *The London Times*, in a review of a performance the day before, raved about Dizzy and two other members of the band, Mickey Roker, drums, and Earl May, bass, the three black artists. The paper reported the other two, Longo and Gafa (the two white musicians) "had absolutely nothing to contribute." The fact was that at least three of the nine selections were composed and arranged by Longo and another one by Gafa.

As Longo later said, "I think he [Dizzy] was playing with their [*The Times'* critics] heads."

Dizzy was equally biting during CORE's (Congress of Racial Equality) efforts in the 1960s to desegregate interstate travel. He is quoted as saying, "We have to play a benefit tonight for the B'nai B'rith and the NAACP. It's sponsored by the John Birch Society, the Ku Klux Klan, the Catholic Youth Organization, and the YMCA, and it's being held in the Greyhound Bus Station in Jackson, Mississippi."

When he witnessed bigotry, Dizzy was not shy even when it came to scolding, if you will, his own as I learned in New York one day. We were in a cab heading for Harlem, when an arranger for Dizzy's band complained about "Jewish landlords" taking advantage of Harlem residents.

"Shut up!" Dizzy shouted at him. The man did not. "I said shut up. Cut that shit out. My man here, Dave, is Jewish. So just shut up. He's my man."

He knew how Jews had suffered in history, and he knew I was sympathetic to the plight of blacks in this country. He also was sensitive to and appreciative of the work Jews had done to assist blacks in their fight for civil rights.

Dizzy considered himself a musician, and politics were not his priority, although he understood, sympathized with, and strongly supported the efforts to fight racism and win blacks all the rights they deserved.

In 1985, while on a trip to Cuba, he reminisced about his youth, stating that he related to poor Cubans because they reminded him of how blacks were oppressed when he grew up. He said, "We couldn't go to white places, we couldn't drink out of white fountains, couldn't go to the libraries or toilets. It was a really, really, bad, bad situation that we came up under. I never liked it…I stayed there because my family was there, and I was small and going to school. But, boy, when I got the chance…"

In discussing the relationship of race and jazz, Hentoff, in his interview with Dizzy, recalled what President Jimmy Carter said when he hosted a concert at the White House to celebrate the 25th anniversary of the Newport (Rhode Island) Jazz Festival.*

President Carter said, "At first, this jazz form was not well accepted in respectable circles. I think there was an element of racism, perhaps at the beginning, because most of the famous early performers were black, and particularly in the South to have black and white musicians playing together was not a normal thing." Then Hentoff noted that even though "no president ever said this before," none of the media reported the remark.

---

*I describe that event and report more of the President's remarks in Chapter 12.

Dizzy was aware of the tremendous progress and improvements in race relations that had occurred in this country. He also knew that racism was not dying easily in the South. He told Hentoff the story that when he was in a New Orleans bar, a man shouted a racial slur at him. When the customer left, the bartender told him, "Remember, for every heel there is a 'soul'." Dizzy said the bartender's overture made him feel better.

Cheraw also was slow to change in race relations. In the Hentoff interview, Dizzy said he visited Cheraw in 1985, and found it still had separate barber shops for whites and blacks. When the black barber shops were busy, he walked into one for whites that had absolutely no customers.

The owner, however, Dizzy told Hentoff, said he did not cut hair for blacks. Dizzy started to leave when the man recognized Dizzy and indicated he would serve him. Dizzy refused the offer and walked out.

Ironically, Dizzy was an invited guest at the Cheraw mayor's home for a reception that evening, and a few days later would be in Myrtle Beach to be inducted into South Carolina's Hall of Fame.

Eventually, like the rest of the South, Cheraw changed. The town that forced Dizzy to attend a segregated school, where he was often vilified as a "niggah," where as a young boy he picked cotton, where he, like all blacks, was denied his dignity, now calls him "Cheraw's most famous son." Signs at the city limits announce that Cheraw is the "home of Dizzy Gillespie." Ten years after his death, on what would have been his 85th birthday in 2003, the city unveiled a seven-foot statue of Dizzy playing his unique horn. The statue stands on the town green. The Cheraw Arts Commission's logo features Dizzy's "bent" horn.

I think Dizzy would have been proud of Cheraw's tributes, not because of the recognition he received, but because it represented progress in the battle against racism, and because of what it meant to African-Americans as a people, his people.

The cause of justice had been served. A dear price had been paid. Blacks were beaten, blood had been spilled, many spent time in prisons, but in the end, blacks won the freedom they had sought and fought for since the days of slavery.

And the tributes from Cheraw, which like most of the South had denigrated blacks, acknowledged that victory.

BAHÁ'í FAITH

11

I was always inspired by Dizzy, the human being: his sensitivity, generosity, his non judgmental character, his desire to bring people together. This was especially true after he converted to the Bahá'i Faith in 1968, about the midway point of our almost 50-year friendship.

Mike Longo, the pianist for Dizzy for more than two decades, told me that Dizzy was introduced to Bahá'i when two of its members, Beth McKenty and her husband, approached Dizzy while he was playing at The Vanguard in Milwaukee in 1966. He agreed to have dinner with them, and the McKentys explained the Bahá'i Faith to him, giving him several pamphlets and a prayer book. After studying and researching the Faith, Dizzy told me he found the Bahá'i friendly, outgoing, and its members comprised of all kinds of people. Most important, he loved that they believed in the betterment of mankind, and that "race unity" was a major priority.

As Dizzy describes his conversion in his autobiography, he was attracted to Bahá'i because of its emphasis on unity. He shared the concept that the world is really one country. The people of the world may be composed of different cultures, races, and ethnicities, and they may speak different languages, but the most important point is that we are one people.

Dizzy would use the following analogy: A painting is created by using different colors — greens, yellows, reds, and many more. They are diverse.

But they are united in the objective to create a beautiful painting. Similarly, the people of the world are diverse, but they should work together to create one beautiful world. He also made the point that all religions basically teach the same lessons, stating, "The teachings of Moses are no different than the teachings of Mohammed."

He supported the concept of diversity but not, he said, at the expense of unity. "Be diverse but don't be diverse and not unified." Dizzy taught his musicians this lesson over and over again. He would warn them that if they decide "…to go out on a limb by yourself," they should think twice before doing so, and "make sure that someone is with you." The instruments of a band or orchestra are diverse — drums, saxophones, trumpets, trombones, violins — but when the musicians play them, they unite to create music.

He said the following after he joined the Bahá'i, "My faith transformed me. I pray every day and my readings intensify my spiritual awareness. As I make a serious effort to fill my life with healthy things, I find I have less and less time for the negative."

When doomsayers would bewail the world and all its sins — wars, corruption, betrayal — Dizzy maintained his faith in mankind. Many believe, he said, that "man is an animal." He disagreed, stating, "man is really noble. He has all the attributes of God himself within, all he has to do is work on it."

In 1973, five years after joining the Bahá'i, he discussed, in depth, his religious beliefs in an interview in London with jazz writer/critic, Les Tomkins.

Tomkins: *It is very obvious that you're essentially a happy man. Presumably, you have a certain philosophy of life that keeps you this way.*

Dizzy: *You're supposed to be joyous creatures here on earth, and if you're anything but joyous, you're not going by what is meant for you. So I try to get as much enjoyment out of life as possible without hurting anyone.*

I belong to the Baha'i Faith…the teaching of 'Abdu'l-Bahá (eldest son of Báha'u'lláh, the founder of the Bahá'i Faith) has strengthened me for five years. You know, one of the hands of the Cause of God says that the next messenger to come, he won't teach by words — it'll be something else. I just learned that today.

Boy, you learn a lot by being around Bahá'is; they hear one of the hands of the cause say something, they remember it, and they repeat it to you. And I do the same thing...they tell me things, I repeat it to people, and they learn things like that. You see, when this religion is over and another prophet comes, before another Cause of God comes on this earth, there will be established a world government. And there will be a universal auxiliary language, spoken by everybody on the face of the globe, taught in every school.

...You know what'll happen — the younger kids that's coming up, they will learn the language, and they will teach the old ones — instead of the other way round. Like now, when the Puerto Ricans come to the United States, they don't speak any English at all. The first words a Puerto Rican child learns in the States is Spanish   but when he hits the street, it's English. You understand what I mean? So they speak beautiful English that they learn at school, and beautiful Spanish from their parents. But their parents speak only broken English. So what will happen with the establishment of this universal language — I can go anywhere in the world. And the world will be one... because there'll be a world government in the first place, and all the laws will be in the universal language.

...That means that people will be communicating on a real heavenly plane. When they understand every word that you say, there's no barriers. If a guy's speaking French and you're speaking English and you don't know what's he's saying, you never get together spiritually. But once that barrier of language is leapt, you start thinking about other ways.

Tomkins: *But what part of this do you think music will play because surely music is already a universal language?*

Dizzy: *Yes it is — already you can get the feeling from music. Well, the music will come into that, too. Like, the same with the part that music played in the Christian revelation. Any music that is written to praise God is good. I don't care what religion it comes under. So there will be, in the future, a groovy number of Bahá'is composing music praising God — heavenly music. That's*

103

what you get when you're dealing in the spirit. We're dealing in spirit now in jazz. Any work that you do praising God is good. Music can transcend the soul to a high level.

Dizzy was, arguably, the most famous member of the Bahá'í Faith at the time, and he touched so many people with his understanding of the Faith. Wherever we traveled in the world, Bahá'í members would come to welcome him, giving him flowers, baskets of fruit or other presents. If the Bahá'í were unable to visit him, they would send the gifts. It was inspiring to see the love they had for Dizzy, and he returned their love in kind.

The creation by Dizzy of the United Nation Orchestra (UNO), composed of artists from several Latin American countries and the U.S., in the late 1980s, reflected his concept of "unity." It merged different kinds of music, and helped achieve Dizzy's objective: to bring people closer together.*

Charlie Fishman, Dizzy's producer and tour manager, perhaps captured the essence of what Dizzy wanted to achieve with the UNO when he observed:

"The concept of the United Nation Orchestra being a family is absolutely reflective of [his] Bahá'í philosophy. The whole idea of that was to bring the music together...the whole vision that Dizzy had was the oneness of humanity. It's one world, we are all its citizens. There is one God, and he has no partners. Dizzy always incorporated this into his speeches because he wanted that message to come across."

There are many Bahá'í centers throughout the world and while Dizzy, given his constant traveling, had little involvement with any of them, he considered himself part of the New York City Bahá'í community. That center on 11th Street between Broadway and University, has named its auditorium the John Birks Gillespie Auditorium. It also displays a huge photo of Dizzy that I donated.

At the recommendation of Mike Longo and Longo's wife, Dorothy (Dottie), and with permission from Lorraine, in January 2004 the center began sponsoring jazz concerts every Tuesday — Jazz Tuesdays — to keep Dizzy's

---

* I write more about the orchestra in Chapter 13.

legacy alive. At the time of this writing, Longo had three bands playing at the center: The Mike Longo Trio; an 18-piece New York State of the Art Jazz Ensemble; and the Mike Longo Funk Band. Longo also books other world-class musicians for the center and once a year in October, the center sponsors a concert celebrating Dizzy which usually highlights trumpeter Jimmy Owens and jazz vocalist Annie Ross. That concert also features a film depicting Dizzy at performances throughout the world. Incidentally, Longo joined the Bahá'i in 1972, and his wife followed in the late '80s.

Dizzy became an emissary for Bahá'u'lláh, who founded the Faith in 19th century Persia, and Dizzy believed uncompromisingly in Bahá'u'lláh's message that, "The Earth is but one country and mankind its citizens, and that the time has come for humanity to live in unity."

THE WHITE HOUSE, JUNE 18, 1978

12

—⊖—

Dizzy did make it to the White House, but not as president, of course. In 1978, President Jimmy Carter hosted a jazz concert to mark the 25th anniversary of the Newport (Rhode Island) Jazz Festival,[*] the first jazz festival in America, founded in 1954.

Dizzy was one of 38 internationally acclaimed jazz musicians who were invited to participate in the celebration of what the White House called "one of the world's foremost musical institutions, the Newport Jazz Festival." In reports of the event, some wrote that this was the largest contingent of world-class jazz artists to appear in one place — ever. It was also the first time a concert devoted entirely to jazz had been held in the White House.[†]

---

[*] The jazz festival moved from Newport to New York in 1972.

[†] The artists who performed, in addition to Dizzy, as listed on the White House program: Benny Carter, alto sax; Ornette Coleman, Stan Getz, Zoot Sims, sax; Dexter Gordon, Illinois Jacquet, Sonny Rollins, tenor sax; Hubie Blake, Chick Corea, Lionel Hampton, Herbie Hancock, Dick Hyman, Cecil Taylor, McCoy Tyner, Mary Lou Williams, Teddy Wilson, piano; Louis Bellson, "Papa" Jo Jones, Max Roach, Tony Williams, drums; Ron Carter, Milt Hinton, bass; Katherine Handy Lewis, vocalist; Doc Cheatham, Roy Eldrige, Clark Terry, trumpet; George Benson, guitar; and Ray Brown, double bass.

Other musicians on the program who were invited but did not perform: Gil Evans, John Lewis, George Russell, Billy Taylor, piano; Gerry Mulligan, Sam Rivers, sax; Mercer Ellington, Joe Newman, trumpet; and Charles Mingus, double bass. The event was produced by George Wein, whom many jazz critics called "the most famous jazz impresario." Wein was also a jazz pianist.

I listed one instrument for each of the artists, but many were proficient in several instruments as well as being vocalists, composers, arrangers, and band leaders.

Besides Dizzy, 28 jazz musicians performed in the concert while another nine were invited as guests. The concert was broadcast live on National Public Radio, and was recorded for broadcast worldwide by the Voice of America.

When Dizzy received the invitation, he called me and asked, "Hey man, wanna go to the White House?" After he explained, of course, I was delighted to have the opportunity. As Dizzy would say, "It ain't every day you get an invite from the prez."

Dizzy was to fly from Los Angeles, California, and I was to meet him in Washington. I couldn't find a commercial flight from Detroit to get me there in time, so I chartered a private plane.

I met Dizzy at the airport where a government limousine picked us up. At the White House gate we encountered a "minor" glitch. I was not on the guest list. Dizzy had not told the proper authorities that he had invited me. He went to work, negotiating with White House security, and, he managed to convince the security personnel to let us — I should say me — in.

It was a special occasion, to say the least. Carter, dressed very casually in a short-sleeved shirt, addressed some 600 guests, stressing the importance of jazz in America's history. In his welcoming remarks, the President said:

"If there ever was an indigenous art form, one that is special and peculiar to the United States and represents what we are as a country, I would say that it's jazz.

"Starting late in the last century, there was a unique combination of two characteristics that have made America what it is: Individuality and a free expression of one's inner spirit in an almost unconstrained way, vivid, alive, aggressive innovative on the one hand, and the severest form of self-discipline on the other, never compromising quality as the human spirit burst forth in an expression of song."

Addressing the issue of jazz and race directly, the President said, "...I believe that this particular form of music, of art, has done as much as anything to break down those (racial) barriers and let us live and work and play and make beautiful music together." Then he continued:

"And the other thing that kind of separated jazz musicians from the upper levels of society was the reputations that jazz musicians had. Some people thought that they stayed up late at night, drank a lot, and did a lot of carousing around, and it took a few years for society to come together.

"I don't know, I'm not going to say as President...(that) jazz musicians became better behaved or the rest of society caught up with them in drinking, carousing around and staying up late at night. But the fact is over a period of a few years, the quality of jazz could not be constrained. It could not be unrecognized, and it swept not only our country, but is perhaps the favorite export product of the United States, and Europe and other parts of the world.

"I began listening to jazz when I was quite young on the radio, listening to performances broadcast from New Orleans. And later when I was a young officer in the Navy in the early '40s, I would go to Greenwich Village to listen to the jazz performers who came there and with my wife, later on, would go down to New Orleans, and listen to individual performances on Sunday afternoons on Royal Street, sit in on the jam sessions that lasted for hours and hours.

"And then later, of course, I began to learn the individual performers through phonograph records and also on the radio itself. This has had a very beneficial effect on my life, and I am very grateful for what all these remarkable performers have done.

"Twenty-five years ago, the first Newport Jazz Festival was held, so this is a celebration of an anniversary and a recognition of what it meant to bring together such a wide diversity of performers, and different elements of jazz in its broader definition that collectively is even a much more profound accomplishment than the superb musicians and individual types of jazz standing alone.

"And it's with a great deal of pleasure that I, as President of the United States, welcome tonight superb representatives of this music form... having performers here who represent the history of music throughout this century, some quite old in years, still young at heart, others newcomers to jazz who brought an increasing dynamism to it and are constantly evolving, striving for perfection as the new elements of jazz are explored."

Each of the musicians "did their thing," as they say in jazz, and you could tell they "gave it a little extra," and when Dizzy finished his solo, he presented the President with a Bahá'i Bible in a beautiful velvet pouch. I could tell that Carter, a religious man, was very moved.

Then Dizzy told me he was ready to leave. I sensed we should stay, that "unscheduled" events after the concert might prove equally fascinating and intriguing. Reluctantly, Dizzy agreed. It would turn out that my instincts were right.

As I was standing with Dizzy, Max Roach, drummer, and Benny Carter, saxophonist, and a few other musicians, I suddenly saw the President, surrounded by Secret Service agents, approach us. Carter tapped Dizzy, who had his back to him, on the shoulder and asked, "How you doin', Diz?"

Dizzy turned and was shocked to see the President. It took Dizzy a second to recover and when he did, he introduced the President to everyone, including Benny Carter. As soon as the President heard the name "Carter" he said, "I know he's one of my folks from the backyard." When the reporters saw this informal gathering, they converged on us with cameras and long boom microphones. Reporters and cameramen were pushing and shoving each other to get close to us.

During what amounted to chit-chat, Carter asked Dizzy if he would perform again. I suggested to Dizzy that he agree, but also insist that the President participate. Dizzy returned to the stage and announced that he had been asked to do "a command performance," and he would comply *only if* the President would join him on stage for a rendition of one of Dizzy's signature pieces, "Salt Peanuts."

"I will not do it unless the President comes up here and sings 'Salt Peanuts'," Dizzy stated firmly. The crowd went wild and the peanut farmer from

Georgia said he would. His wife, Rosalynn, had, by this time, joined the President.

"Salt Peanuts" has no lyrics. The band and its leader yell out "salt peanuts" twice very quickly at different spots in the piece. The President, with no coaching, carried off his part perfectly, shouting "salt peanuts" six times at the appropriate time, and the crowd roared. In fact, Roach helped the President a little bit with timing by giving him a signal with his drumstick. On the sixth repetition, the President chuckled and couldn't finish.

Dizzy laughed so hard I thought he would fall off the bandstand. After the President finished, Dizzy yelled out to the crowd, "I just want to ask one question...I want to ask one question. Would you like to go on the road with us?" To which Carter replied, "I might have to after tonight."

In reporting on the President's solo, the *Christian Science Monitor*, wrote: "His [President Carter's] singing of the bebop classic, 'Salt Peanuts', gave

President Carter performing "Salt Peanuts" with Dizzy and Max Roach on drums, June 18, 1978. *Photo courtesy of Jimmy Carter Presidential Library.*

the evening a climax perhaps impossible to surpass." Then the paper added humorously, "Well, maybe 'singing' is too strong a word."

The *Akron Beacon Journal* stated in its headline, "Singer Carter Stops Show," writing in the story that "...his [Carter's] performance left his accompanist trumpeter Dizzy Gillespie in stitches and unable to continue." As I remember, Dizzy completed the piece with Max Roach on drums.

In a serious vein, the *Christian Science Monitor* said, "...this was an event in the history of American music."

Back in our rooms at the L'Enfant Plaza Hotel, we turned on all our TV sets — we had three in two adjoining rooms — in order to watch the newscasts on all the channels because we expected major coverage, given the President's impromptu participation on stage. We were not disappointed. It was the lead story on several stations.

That's me recording a conversation between President Carter and Dizzy at the 25th Anniversary of the Newport (Rhode Island) Jazz Festival in the White House June 18, 1978. *Photo courtesy of Jimmy Carter Presidential Library.*

NBC News anchor, John Chancellor, in reporting on the event, did not mention the President by name. He simply said there was a "jazz party" at the White House last night. "There was a singer. He sang a song called 'Salt Peanuts.' Watch closely." Then he played the tape of the President's performance with Dizzy.

An interesting twist to the story was that John Wilson, the famous jazz critic at *The New York Times*, left right after the concert and before President Carter's performance. The country's "paper of record" did not report this piece of jazz history in its first edition. Journalists use "30" on their copy to indicate the end of their story, and Wilson had "thirtied" out a little too early. I don't know how the paper did it, but Carter's "Salt Peanuts" performance was reported in later editions.

Had we left when Dizzy finished his part in the concert, we wouldn't have made jazz history with the President of the United States.

WHITE HOUSE VISIT AND THE KENNEDY CENTER HONOR

13

—O—

Dizzy enjoyed another visit to the White House when he was awarded the National Medal of Arts by President George H.W. Bush on the recommendation of the National Endowment of the Arts (NEA) in November 1989.

This was the event that the composer and conductor, Leonard Bernstein, boycotted, refusing the award to protest NEA's cancellation of a $10,000 grant to a controversial New York City gallery exhibit about AIDS. The furor arose over an exhibition, "Witnesses: Against Our Vanishing" at Arts Space, a Manhattan art gallery and arts activist organization. The cancellation of the grant resulted because the show was considered too sexually explicit and the catalogues describing the exhibit were also critical of some public officials.

Bernstein asked Dizzy to protest as well, but Dizzy refused. I thought it was wrong of Bernstein; it was *meshugeh* (crazy). He should never have made, what I considered, an outrageous request. Although Bernstein, before the event, apologized publicly, he was not re-invited and he was not in attendance at the ceremony. After negotiations with Arts Space, the NEA restored the grant.

In addition to Dizzy, 11 others were honored. They were: writers John Updike and Czeslaw Milosz; painter Robert Motherwell; choreographer Katherine Dunham; arts patron Leigh Gerdine; sculptor Walker Kirtland Hancock; art center director Martin Friedman; preservationist Leopold Adler; the Dayton Hudson Corp., of Minneapolis; photographer Alfred Eisenstaedt; and pianist Vladimir Horowitz.

We flew to D.C. from a gig in Brazil,* and Dizzy was tired after our long, all-night flight. It had been an arduous trip to Washington to make it in time for the event. He was sitting in the first row in the East Room, waiting to receive his medal, and when they called his name, Dizzy was dozing. I was sitting right behind him, and I had to nudge him to wake him up.

Dizzy was honored "for his trail-blazing work as a musician who helped elevate jazz to an art form of the first rank, and for sharing his gift with listeners around the world."

At the ceremony, John E. Frohnmayer, NEA chairman, said, "John Birks 'Dizzy' Gillespie is a virtuoso musician, pioneer, composer, and bandleader who has been a pivotal figure in 20th century American music. The founder of the jazz bebop movement, he developed a radical new approach to improvisation that was to change the course of modern music-making. For more than 40 years, he has explored the varied music of different cultures. Mr. Gillespie has performed before countless world leaders and has won numerous awards."

Then, just before the President hung the medal around Dizzy's neck, Dizzy felt something was askew. He had not zippered his pants. Without missing a beat, Dizzy zipped his pants with President Bush and the First Lady Barbara Bush, and many famous, powerful and distinguished guests in the audience looking on. I think it is safe to say no one ever, in the history of the world, zipped up before such prominent people or at such a formal occasion. Dizzy was dizzier than usual that day.

(Perhaps not quite as embarrassing, Dizzy's middle name "Birks" was misspelled in the program. It was spelled with an "e.")

---

*I discuss the 1989 trip to Brazil in the next chapter.

Dizzy zipping up in front of President Bush (41) and First Lady Barbara Bush when Dizzy was awarded the National Medal of Arts in 1989.

I "saved" a bundle of money that day when I had my photo taken with President Bush and his wife. I was told that under usual circumstances such a photo cost $5,000.

The following year, 1990, I was privileged to join Dizzy when he received the lifetime achievement award from the Kennedy Center for the Performing Arts, probably the country's most prestigious event in recognizing the work of artists. Dizzy was honored that night along with Katharine Hepburn, actress; Rise Stevens, opera singer; Jule Styne, composer; and Billy Wilder, director.

I attended the event and was accompanied by Dave Heard, brother of jazz drummer J.C. Heard, and Eddie Bierman, a lifelong friend who worked with me at Dee Gee. We had a somewhat embarrassing moment when we arrived by limousine. We stepped out of the car onto the red carpet, and after taking a few steps, the fans, standing behind ropes, broke out in applause.

The three of us were somewhat taken aback by the recognition but enjoyed a boost to our egos until…we saw Katharine Hepburn walking ahead of us.

As much as we might have wanted to believe the applause was for us, we didn't fool ourselves and, we returned to earth very quickly.

Dizzy's good friend, the well-known and beloved comedian, Bill Cosby, narrated Dizzy's lifetime achievements in typical Cosby form. Talking about Dizzy's penchant for sarcasm, particularly when racism was the subject, Cosby said he was with Dizzy in France when Dizzy played at a jazz festival.

Cosby said somebody came by with a tray of watermelon and Dizzy said, "Hmmm, a letter from home." "And my wife…said, 'Make sure you spit out the stamps.'"

Cosby said that when he informed Dizzy that the members of the 18-piece band playing, "A Night in Tunisia," a Gillespie classic, were Japanese, Dizzy replied, "That's funny. They don't sound Japanese."

Cosby made a special point of paying tribute to Dizzy for creating the United Nation Orchestra* in the 1980s. It was a 15-member orchestra composed of: three Brazilians, three Cubans, six Americans, one Panamanian, one Dominican and one Puerto Rican. Dizzy's idea was to bring different music cultures together and create one "world family of music." The orchestra had its premiere performance in 1988.

Alyn Shipton, a jazz critic, in his biography on Dizzy, *Groovin' High*, *The Life of Dizzy Gillespie*, observed that this band was Dizzy's "crowning achievement as a leader…" Shipton wrote:

> "His supreme achievement of the late 1980s was to be his United Nation Orchestra, a musical melting pot that combined the rhythmical and emotional charge he felt for the music of Brazil and Cuba, with the harmonic and melodic idea he had himself introduced to jazz."

At dinner, I told Dizzy I felt awkward sitting at his table with his family and the other prominent, world-famous people at such a prestigious event.

---

* It was named by Lalo Schifrin and it had no connection to the United Nations which has its own orchestra.

Stating I was to stay put because I was right where I should be, he responded, "Hey man, this is *the* family's table." I never forgot that. It touched me deeply.

I was privileged to visit the White House again when President Bill Clinton invited Lorraine to the 40th anniversary celebration of the Newport Jazz Festival in June 1993, 15 years after President Carter paid tribute to that classic jazz event, and six months after Dizzy died.*

Lorraine could not attend because of health reasons; she suffered from a variety of serious allergies, and she asked me to represent her. I was more than happy to do so.

What I remember most is that, in his remarks, President Clinton captured the essence of what the Newport Jazz Festival has meant to this country, and what jazz has meant to the world. He said at the ceremony:

"No event has done more to nurture the career of jazz artists; none has done more to thrill and delight jazz fans. The festival's influence has been truly profound, inspiring more than 2,000 other jazz festivals every year around the world."

In concluding his speech, President Clinton said, "...jazz is the true reflection of the American people, a music of inclusion, a music of democracy, a music that embraces tradition, and the freedom to innovate."

As Dizzy would have said, with a blast of a high C on his horn, "Yea man, amen."

---

*President Clinton's daily schedule, which we received in our research on the event, mistakenly refers to the celebration as the 14th anniversary of the festival.

TRAVELING WITH DIZZY

14

—❖—

Dizzy was on the road constantly. He moved all the time. I doubt that in any one year he was at home in Englewood, New Jersey more than a few weeks or so. He visited every corner of the world, and he received warm welcomes wherever he went.

Taking a snooze on a bus while heading from one gig to the next. *Photo courtesy of Dany Gignoux.*

Consider: Several biographies of Dizzy report that in 1989 alone he performed more than 300 times in 27 countries, as well as in 100 U.S. cities in 31 states, and Washington, D.C.

In keeping an unbelievable schedule, he said he'd rather feel tired than bored. And when he went somewhere "significant," he would ask me to tag along, and if I could get away from my business at Marine Pollution Control, I would do all that was possible to join him.

One of those "significant" trips was to Cuba in 1985. Dizzy had visited Cuba in 1977 after President Carter lifted travel restrictions to Cuba. Dizzy welcomed the change in U.S. foreign policy as it related to Cuba, writing in his autobiography, that he wanted to play *with* people not *against* them. He emphasized he was making his comments on an "artistic level" not on a political one.

It was on the 1977 visit that he met Cuba's famous jazz trumpeter, Arturo Sandoval. Sandoval had heard about Dizzy visiting Cuba and went to meet him. He volunteered to drive Dizzy around Havana, taking him into black neighborhoods where the natives played guaguancó and rumba. Sandoval did not reveal that he was a jazz musician himself. When he finally did, he and Dizzy performed together in Cuba, and Sandoval became a Dizzy protégé.

Regarding his effort to meet Dizzy, Sandoval was quoted as saying, "I went to the boat to find him [Dizzy.] I've never had a complex about meeting famous people. If I respect somebody, I go there and try to meet them."

After the 1977 visit, Sandoval occasionally toured the U.S. to perform with Dizzy, and, of course, he was always "shadowed" by Cuban officials who were assigned to assure that Sandoval would not defect. About 13 years later, Dizzy would be part of an intricate plan that led to the successful defection of Sandoval to the U.S.

The 1985 tour had two objectives: Dizzy would play at Havana's Fifth International Jazz Festival, and participate in the production of a documentary of Dizzy's tour.

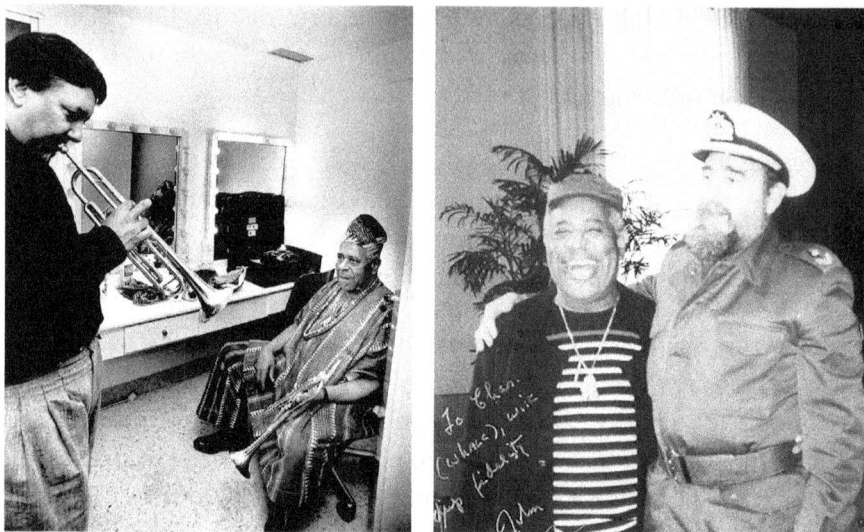

Left: Dizzy in his African garb with trumpeter Arturo Sandoval, whom Dizzy helped defect from Cuba. Dizzy asked Sandoval: "How did you get that sound? You must have had a famous professor!" Sandoval replied, "Me? No, I learned on the streets…" *Photo courtesy of Dany Gignoux*. *Right*: Fidel Castro, Cuba's leader, drapes arm around Dizzy.

Dizzy in Cuba (1985) with photos of Fidel Castro *(left)* and his brother, Raúl, on the wall.

Although travel restrictions had been eased, Cuba still had strict clearance measures in place, which did not make it easy for us. While Dizzy, for obvious reasons, was not subject to a major inspection, I was. Before leaving from Miami, the plane was held up because my papers had not been delivered by the Swiss government which handled such clearances since the U.S. did not have diplomatic relations with Cuba.

The producer of the documentary, Nim Polanetska, brought her own film crew which followed us everywhere as the Cuban authorities took us to hospitals, a factory that produced cigars, another one that manufactured musical equipment, and other sites chosen by the Cuban government to show off its best assets. We stayed at Hotel Nacional de Cuba and visited the famous night club, Trocadero.

We did not meet Fidel Castro, Cuba's dictator, during the tour, but just when we were ready to leave, Dizzy received a message that Castro wanted to see him. We waited...and waited...and waited...for Castro's people to pick us up. I became impatient and went to buy souvenirs. I was on my shopping spree when government officials arrived, and took Dizzy and the band to Castro's offices. Unfortunately, I missed the opportunity to meet Castro then, although I would see Castro five years later when Dizzy performed in Namibia to help that country celebrate its independence.

An 85-minute documentary of the 1985 trip, produced by Cubana Bop Partners, a U.S. company, entitled "A Night in Havana: Dizzy Gillespie in Cuba," was released in the U.S. by the New Video Group, Inc. in 1989.

The film was well-received, but *The New York Times* wrote, "Although this... film is nicely made and the music is wonderful and overpowering, it could not overpower the ill-conceived pandering praises which with [sic] Gillespie embraced Castro and his regime...Unfortunately, Dizzy, that wonderful, creative, musical genius, will persist in our minds bear-hugging a cigar-chomping dictator in starched, olive-green fatigues."

I could not believe the criticism. The paper missed the entire point. This was not about politics. This was about music, the universal language. A major objective of freedom and democracy is that we try to understand each other. In short, the criticism, I felt and still do years later, was unconscionable.

Dizzy addressed the issue of what he hoped his music would achieve while speaking at a performance one night. Reading from prepared remarks, which was unusual for Dizzy, he stated: "We are here tonight to demonstrate what one brother can give to the other in a spirit of unity. If our respective governments cannot join hands in the spirit of brotherly love, we will demonstrate to them how..."

Castro gave Dizzy several gifts, including four boxes of Cuban cigars, and a stuffed alligator. (The shape of Cuba resembles an alligator.) After getting off our chartered plane in Miami, Dizzy had the gifts on a wheelie, but hadn't completed the custom cards declaring them. When the custom officer saw all the gifts, recognized Dizzy, and knew about the trip, and not wanting to deal with the issue, he yelled at Dizzy to "get out of here."

The effort to help Sandoval defect started five years after we returned from the 1985 visit.

Dizzy enjoying a few playful minutes with children during his visit to Cuba in 1985.

125

I was not directly involved, but here is what I learned from interviews Berl conducted with Charlie Fishman, Dizzy's personal manager and producer, who with the help of a top White House official, David C. Miller, Jr., organized Sandoval's escape.*

In February 1990, Dizzy, accompanied by Fishman, visited Cuba once more for the Havana International Jazz Festival. Dizzy, Fishman and Charlie "Whale" Lake, Dizzy's tour manager, were housed in a fancy villa in a Havana suburb. One day, Sandoval came to the villa, and asked Fishman to follow him outside; he wanted to discuss an important private matter. Once comfortable that they could not be overheard, Sandoval told Fishman that he and his family wanted to defect to the U.S., and asked for help.

Fishman relayed Sandoval's request to Dizzy, who told Fishman they should and would do whatever was necessary to assist Sandoval. The cloak-and-dagger execution of the plan took place over the next five months.

At one point, I was with Dizzy when he called former First Lady Nancy Reagan to enlist her help with Sandoval's defection. Dizzy told Nancy Reagan that Sandoval wanted to defect, adding Sandoval would not do so without his wife, Marianela, and son, Arturo Sandoval III, who was 12 at the time. Could she help?

Dizzy had established a relationship with Ronald Reagan and his wife when they were still in Hollywood before they occupied the White House between 1981 and 1988. I am confident that the call helped get the ball rolling, although the defection occurred in mid-1990, during the administration of President George H.W. Bush, who took office in 1989.

When Sandoval made his family's desire to defect known to Fishman, Sandoval was already scheduled to join a month-long summer tour of Europe with Dizzy's United Nation Orchestra (UNO), beginning in late June 1990. An elaborate plot was hatched in concert with Sandoval's manager, Peter King, who was based in London. In addition to the UNO dates with

---

*Berl tried numerous times to interview Arturo Sandoval, but Sandoval, while indicating in e-mails that he was prepared to tell his story for this book, never made himself available.

Dizzy, King organized a long "phantom" tour in Europe that had Sandoval performing for an extended period following the UNO tour.

Sandoval told Cuban authorities that he was not willing to be away from his family for such a long time, and received permission to have his wife and son spend the summer in London with King and his family, so that he could visit them between engagements.

The plan involved the White House, and the U.S. embassies in Athens and Rome. Fishman, before leaving for the European tour, contacted Miller, special assistant to the president for National Security Affairs, whom he and Dizzy had met when they flew with then-Secretary of State James Baker, to Namibia to join in celebrating that country's road to independence in March 1990.* After establishing a rapport, Fishman told Miller of Sandoval's desire to defect. Miller pledged his support and gave Fishman his business card.

Fishman sent the tour itinerary to Miller who arranged an appointment for Fishman, Dizzy and Sandoval at the U.S. embassy in Greece when the UNO would spend three days there in July 1990. At the embassy, Sandoval applied for asylum.

Somehow, Cuban authorities got wind of Sandoval's intentions, and immediately instructed him to leave the tour and return to Havana with his wife and son. Sandoval was frightened. Late one night, in Varese, Italy, Sandoval, accompanied by fellow Cubans, Paquito D'Rivera, UNO co-musical director who had defected from Cuba in 1981 while on a tour in Spain, and Ignacio Berroa, Dizzy's drummer, went to Dizzy's and Fishman's suite. Sandoval was in a panic. Dizzy was asleep. Fishman called Miller at the White House, but Miller was home with his family.

Thus began a round of phone calls between Fishman and American officials that culminated in Fishman being instructed to take Sandoval to Rome the following morning.

Miller, in an interview with us, said he received a phone call at about 2 a.m. from the Situation Room in the White House. The White House contact told

---

*I discuss that trip later in this chapter.

Miller that a telephone call came in asking for him [Miller], and it "involved something about a man named Dizzy Gillespie. They thought it might be a crank call."

Chuckling about the phone call from the Situation Room, Miller said in our interview that he immediately contacted the Rome embassy and said it had the support of the White House in facilitating the defection of Sandoval. Then, he said, he went to the White House to "watch over the operation."

In Rome, Dizzy's entourage was met by U.S. government officials on the tarmac. Sandoval remained in an embassy vehicle as Fishman went to retrieve luggage. They were whisked to the U.S. embassy where arrangements were made to fly Sandoval to the States. Meanwhile, Sandoval's wife and son were instructed to go to the U.S. embassy in London, and they were flown to the U.S. at almost the same time Sandoval took off from Rome. Fishman told us he lent Sandoval the money for the airline ticket to the U.S.

The entire plan was very well coordinated, Fishman said. As I indicated, I had no idea how all this was accomplished, but I am convinced that Dizzy's call to Nancy Reagan led to important political support for the mission. Fishman, however, told Berl he had no knowledge of Dizzy's call to Nancy Reagan. Miller said he also was unaware that Dizzy had reached out to the former First Lady.

After the defection was carried out successfully, Miller said he received a note from President Bush, stating, "Good work."

Sandoval became a U.S. citizen, and star jazz musician in the U.S., and his story was told in a made-for-cable movie, "For Love of Country: The Arturo Sandoval Story." At one point, Sandoval played with the Detroit Symphony Orchestra, and I introduced him to the musicians.

Another memorable trip was to Nigeria. It happened that I was on a business trip in Nigeria in January 1989 when Dizzy visited the country as part of a United States Information Agency tour. The tour would also include Zaire, Senegal, Egypt and Morocco. The Nigerian visit would be very emotional for Dizzy because he learned years earlier that his family roots went deep into that African country. His great-great grandfather had been a chief in West

Africa. He lived in northern Nigeria, and his given name was Iwo. (Dizzy named his music publishing company "Iwo".) His great grandmother was a daughter of a Yoruba tribal chief. So the Nigerian tour touched Dizzy deeply.

He was honored by the Nigerians and installed as a tribal chief of Iperu, a town near the Ibu River in the Ogun State in southwestern Nigeria. During the elaborate ceremony, Dizzy wore a green, beige and white African costume that the natives had given him as a gift. (It weighed 42 pounds.) He took off his shoes and danced with the others in the red dirt to sacred drumming and chanting.

I don't think I ever saw him so emotional. He talked about that trip and ceremony many times. It left a lasting mark on him which, of course, was understandable given that it involved his heritage.

In discussing our travels, Dizzy said there were three places he wanted to visit: Bahia in Brazil, China, and Bora Bora in the South Pacific. He never made it to China or Bora Bora but he did get to Bahia, and I joined him on that trip as well.

Members of Dizzy's band and me in Nigeria in 1989. *Left to right*: Ed Cherry, guitar; John Lee, bass; me; Ignacio Berroa, drums; and James Moody, sax.

We had been in Brazil during the famous 1956 South American tour sponsored by the U.S. State Department, but we did not make it to Bahia on that occasion. In missing that opportunity, Dizzy wrote in his autobiography:

"We didn't get a chance to go to Bahia and missed seeing the real black part of Brazil. We saw a lot of blacks, but not a heavy concentration like you'd probably see in Bahia, which is the area where most of the creativity of the arts and music comes from."

Dizzy and me in our African costumes given to us in Nigeria where Dizzy was installed as a tribal chief of Iperu in 1989.

He had another opportunity to visit Bahia when he had a gig in Brazil in 1989.

Before his live performance, Dizzy had an engagement at a major Rio television station. We arrived in a taxi, went into the building and prepared for the show when... Dizzy discovered he had left his trumpet, his special trumpet, in the taxi's trunk.

Dizzy panicked a bit because it was important to him that he played his own instrument. We called the police and contacted the cab company. A major search was launched. To our surprise, they found the trumpet in less than an hour, and the police delivered it. To this day, I don't know how they did it. At the time, I don't believe the cabs had two-way radios. Despite the fact that Dizzy was still somewhat upset, the show was aired without incident.

Regarding Bahia, Dizzy wanted to visit the city in the northeastern part of the country because it had a history similar to that of the U.S. in practicing slavery. Slaves arrived in Bahia from Africa, and then were sent to different parts of the country to work in the sugar cane fields. It was the site of a slave rebellion in 1835. Dizzy knew a little about the slave trade in Bahia and wanted to learn more.

When word spread about his interest in visiting Bahia, a man who sang at a club in Bahia said he would take us; he would be our guide. As a matter of fact, Dizzy had played for a few minutes on a recording this man had produced sometime earlier, and the man had paid Dizzy for his participation. Dizzy agreed, and we flew to Bahia.

After leaving the airport by car, Dizzy stopped periodically to join locals he saw drinking and playing dominos along the highway by the sea.

Dizzy loved to mingle with people. He was welcomed warmly and, Dizzy graciously accepted the hospitality. Ignoring my warnings, he drank with them. Specifically, he was drinking kahshahsah. I had no idea what was in the drink. I had never heard of it. Who knew what the drink contained? Dizzy was enjoying himself as he played dominos with the men, and I recall that he had two or three glasses of this native drink.

The guide took us to a club, the Meridian, housed in an auditorium in our hotel where Dizzy performed for about 20 minutes. Then, to our amazement, we discovered the guide had sold tickets with Dizzy's name on them. We didn't know that he had promoted Dizzy's appearance to make a fast buck. Dizzy and I realized, too late, that we had been hustled.

Later that night, in addition to being burned by the Bahia singer, Dizzy suffered the aftermath of drinking kahshahsah. I heard a knock at my hotel room at about 2 a.m. It was Dizzy.

"I don't know what's wrong," he said. "I feel rotten."

I can't say it was totally unexpected considering the drinks he'd consumed, and I was worried. I called the hotel desk and asked them to send a doctor. I don't know what the doctor did, but Dizzy was fine in the morning.

I think Dizzy was ill, not just from the drink, but he was also very upset that the singer who took us to Bahia had taken advantage of him. I noticed Dizzy became very sad when he realized what had happened at the club. Dizzy had an innate trust in humans, and when wronged, it hurt him immensely.

In hindsight, I often thought maybe he was already ill with the cancer that took his life a little more than three years later. Perhaps his illness in Bahia was a sign that cancer was already in his body. I don't know, but I thought about it often. Maybe if we had known earlier…just maybe, he could have been treated successfully. Who knows?

Another African trip that I cherished came a little more than a year later when I accompanied Dizzy to Namibia in March 1990. Namibia was celebrating its independence after a 26-year struggle with South Africa against which it had rebelled. Dizzy was to perform at the state independence banquet. This was a very auspicious occasion. Dizzy and Fishman were invited by then-Secretary of State James Baker to travel with his entourage on his plane. I flew commercial from London where I was on MPC business. (It was on this trip that Charlie Fishman met David Miller, the special assistant to the president who helped carry out the defection of Sandoval.)

Part of Namibia's celebration was held in a sports arena. Another event, the state banquet, was attended by several dozen of the world's major leaders, including Egyptian President Hosni Mubarak; Fidel Castro, Cuba's leader; Nelson Mandela, the South African anti-apartheid activist who would serve as South Africa's first black president, and who had been released from prison just six weeks earlier; Javier Pérez de Cuéllar, the secretary general of the United Nations; F.W. de Klerk, who was president of South Africa during its apartheid days; Bishop Desmond Tutu, the famous Anglican social rights activist; and many others.

I might point out that Bishop Tutu sat at the table with Dave Usher. I mean I sat at the table with the bishop, and it was table No. 33, my lucky number which popped up constantly in my life. Dizzy was also at the same table.

132

It was, to say the least, awe-inspiring to be in the midst of all these leaders. Here was a "nice Jewish boy," who once spread oil on gravel roads to keep the dust down, sitting with some of the most influential rulers in the world. Of course, it was not my own achievements that brought me there. I was able to rub shoulders with the most powerful in the world because of my relationship with a world-famous musician loved by those in attendance and their constituencies.

Dizzy, wearing the African costume he had been given in Nigeria, was, as always, phenomenal. I thought if only that music could help all these leaders create peace in the world. Here they were laughing and cheering while they listened to some of the best jazz in the world. For a few hours, they forgot about the differences they had with each other, differences that sometimes led to war.

Left to right: Nelson Mandela, South Africa's anti-apartheid activist and its first black president; me (in background); Dizzy; and Nigeria's Prime Minister Hage Geinbog at Namibia's celebration of its independence, March 1990.

Dizzy and me at Table No. 33 (my lucky number) at Namibia's independence celebration in 1990. Dizzy performed at the ceremonies.

CANCER: THE LOSS
OF A JAZZ GIANT

15

—⊖—

"Man, I don't feel so good."

That was Dizzy's complaint to me about an hour after I picked him up in early December 1991 at the Detroit Metropolitan Airport for an appearance with the Detroit Symphony Orchestra (DSO.)

Dizzy was scheduled to perform December 6 in celebration of the 50th anniversary of the Paradise Theatre where, as I wrote in Chapter One, I met Dizzy some 47 years earlier in 1944 when I was 14 years old. Also on the program at the DSO was jazz pianist Mike Longo, who would perform "A World of Gillespie," which Dizzy had commissioned him to write, and which had premiered at the Henry Street Settlement House in New York a year earlier.

(Dizzy was scheduled to play the piece with the London Philharmonic Orchestra in 1986. After spending thousands of dollars in New York to make copies of the sheet music for all the musicians, Dizzy discovered, upon arrival in London, that he was not alone on the program and there was not enough time to play Longo's composition.)

I was concerned about Dizzy. I called the DSO and asked for a doctor. Longo shared my feelings, telling me Dizzy had complained about pain in his testicles and that he would sit in his room and just stare.

Dr. Clyde Wu, a DSO board member and a medical doctor, examined Dizzy in my Marine Pollution Control's offices on Jefferson. Understandably reluctant to make a specific diagnosis at MPC, Dr. Wu nevertheless strongly recommended that Dizzy return home and see his doctor. I don't know what Dr. Wu thought was wrong, but he was obviously concerned, particularly when he learned that after Detroit, Dizzy was headed to Japan. Dizzy tried to pay Dr. Wu, but Dr. Wu kindly refused payment.*

Dizzy had another physical examination in my apartment near the Detroit River by a doctor from the insurance company that was covering his overseas trips. This doctor didn't indicate any concern; Dizzy passed the examination.

At the DSO performance, The Dizzy Gillespie Quintet, which included Dizzy, John Lee, bass; Ed Cherry, guitar; Ron Holloway, tenor sax; and Ignacio Berroa, drums, was outstanding. Longo told me that Dizzy played with such vigor that his concerns abated.

Interestingly, also on the program that evening, was the band leader, Cab Calloway, with whom Dizzy played early in his career. Dizzy was a member of Calloway's band when he had a much-reported altercation with Calloway in which Dizzy slashed Calloway with a knife in 1941.

The band was playing at the State Theater in Hartford, Connecticut, when a spitball landed next to Calloway, who accused Dizzy of throwing it. Dizzy denied the charge (in fact, he did not throw it), and the two had a scuffle during which Dizzy drew a knife. Bassist Milton Hinton deflected the knife which, nevertheless, cut Calloway in the buttocks. Calloway fired Dizzy on the spot.

The two reconciled in later years, yet I sensed tension when they met at the DSO. Calloway, acting as if Dizzy was still a member of his band and his employee, looked at his watch and told Dizzy, "You're late." Dizzy, to his

---

*Dr. Wu, head of the DSO's jazz teaching program, the only one of its kind among symphony orchestras in the U.S., along with DSO Director Jack A. Robinson, founder and former chairman of Perry Drug Stores, Inc., which before being acquired by Rite Aid Corporation, was the largest drugstore chain in Michigan, were the ones who sponsored me to become a DSO board member, a position I have held since 1998, and which I value very much.

credit, let the remark pass without comment. I think he showed his usual class.

Ignoring Dr. Wu's warning, Dizzy insisted on keeping his performance schedule. Berl, in talking to Charlie Fishman, Dizzy's personal manager and producer at the time, and Charlie "Whale" Lake, Dizzy's tour manager for 18 years, pieced together the chronology of Dizzy's illness, which led to his having the exploratory surgery that revealed he was suffering from pancreatic cancer.

After Dizzy's Detroit appearance, Dizzy, along with Fishman, traveled to Japan where Fishman noticed Dizzy was not himself. He was sleeping much later than usual, and not taking his traditional walk or reading the papers. Fishman tried to talk Dizzy out of going to Houston, Texas, the next scheduled stop, reminding Dizzy of his busy schedule in the coming year (1992) which included a 75th birthday bash and tribute, and several concerts around the world.

Dizzy refused to cancel any appearances and played for three nights in Houston where Fishman noticed the same strange behavior Dizzy had exhibited in Japan. Houston was followed by "Dizzy's Diamond Jubilee," a month-long engagement at the Blue Note in New York, followed by a solo appearance in Alabama. One night, Fishman found Dizzy throwing up. Dizzy attributed his condition to "something I ate."

Fishman flew home while Dizzy was off to Scottsdale, Arizona, where Lake, who was with Dizzy, said that after visiting a synagogue, Dizzy became very ill in his hotel room, filling his sink in the bathroom with vomit. Still, Dizzy refused help, and would not cancel upcoming performances. He continued on to Kimball's East Jazz Club in Emeryville, California northwest of Oakland, where, on opening night, he collapsed on his way up to the stage.

"I can't make it, man," Lake said Dizzy told him. "The look in his eyes was eerie, scary."

Lake called for help from the audience, asking specifically if there was a doctor in the house, and a woman doctor responded. She examined Dizzy and said he needed to be hospitalized which he immediately was. Doctors treated him for his diabetes which Dizzy had contracted as an adult in 1985. Lake said Dizzy's diabetes "had exploded." After four days in the hospital, Dizzy demanded to be released. He went back to Kimball's and played for five nights before heading to Seattle for a week-long scheduled appearance at Dimitriou's Jazz Alley.

Fishman, who was kept abreast of Dizzy's health, was concerned and flew to Seattle. During the last week in February, Dizzy called Fishman into the bathroom, and pointed to his urine "which was orange." Fishman strongly urged Dizzy to be checked out by a doctor.

Reluctantly Dizzy agreed, canceling scheduled appearances in Argentina, London, and Paris. He also canceled a concert in South Africa, where he was to perform with the legendary Miriam Makeba whose patron — South Africa's anti-apartheid hero Nelson Mandela — Dizzy had met at Namibia's celebration of its independence in March 1990, only two years earlier.

Dizzy flew home to Englewood where, in the Englewood Hospital and Medical Center, his pancreatic cancer was discovered during exploratory surgery on March 12, 1992.

Although I had received reports throughout Dizzy's travels that he was not doing well, I was stunned by the diagnosis because I knew that pancreatic cancer was usually terminal. It was not easy news to digest. My brother, my friend, the jazz artist without equal, was going to die.

I visited him in the hospital many times during the next 11 months, and each time he looked thinner and weaker. The last time I saw him, three days before he died, I gave him a suede hat which, while smiling broadly, he put on his head with the brim on the right side. He still displayed his humor, even under these dire circumstances.

After that visit, I returned to Detroit, and I was not at his bedside when he died January 6, 1993. I received a call from Mike Longo that Dizzy was gone. His death from the wretched disease was inevitable, yet it still was a shock. One is never prepared to accept such a tremendous loss. It is impossible to develop emotional and psychological protective mechanisms to guard against the resultant grief. One is never "prepared."

Two memorials were held for Dizzy in New York. The first was private at Saint Peter's Church on Lexington and East 54th Street. The church commits much of its programming to jazz. The other, at the Cathedral Church of Saint John the Divine on Amsterdam between 110th and 112th Streets, was public and attended by thousands.

At the open casket, I was taken aback because Dizzy was wearing a Marine Pollution Control tie with the red anchor logo. He would be buried in it. I believe that Lorraine along with some of Dizzy's family members, recognizing Dizzy's close friendship with me, made the arrangements to have Dizzy wear the tie. In fact, Dizzy frequently wore a cap with the MPC logo at many performances, which was one way he expressed how much he valued our friendship. Lorraine, a few days after Dizzy's death, sent me a couple of Dizzy's jackets that I had worn while on the road with Dizzy. She knew that Dizzy and I frequently exchanged jackets as our respective weights went up and down. It was a very kind gesture on Lorraine's part. Dizzy was buried in Flushing Cemetery, Queens, New York.

I was touched by the family's thoughtfulness. The family gave me another honor at the funeral open to the public when it made sure that, although there were some 40 pallbearers, I would be at the front of the casket, the first one. The other pallbearer across from me at the front was Sir George Shearing , the jazz pianist, who was knighted for his achievements in music in 2007.

The Bahá'i also paid tribute to the world famous member of its faith. The international governing body of the Bahá'i Faith, the Universal House of Justice, issued the following statement upon Dizzy's death:

"We share your great sorrow at the passing of dearly loved, highly cherished John Birks Gillespie whose steadfastness in the Cause of Baha'u'llah and constant promotion of its teachings added a luminous quality and enviable dimension to the far-reaching influence of his distinguished life. Our grateful memory of his Bahá'i services is ineradicable. We ardently pray at the Holy Threshold for the progress of his radiant soul throughout the divine worlds. Kindly convey our loving sympathy to his dear wife Lorraine."

The American Bahá'í newspaper published a long obituary on Dizzy. Under the headline, "Farewell, Diz," the paper reported that, "Mr. Gillespie, a Bahá'í since 1968, proclaimed the Cause of God in cities, towns and villages all over the world, winning the hearts of everyone from European royalty to African villages…with the warmth and humor even as he amazed them with the brilliance of technical facility of a trumpet style that made him one of the most honored and respected jazz musicians of the 20th Century."

Attending the funeral were representatives of the International Bahá'í Community, the National Spiritual Assembly, and the Spiritual Assembly of New York City. Techeste Ahderom, representative to the United Nations for the Bahá'í International Community, delivered messages of praise and condolences from Bahá'í communities in Jamaica, France, and Austria.

In 1997, Longo, who was at Dizzy's bedside when he died and delivered one of the eulogies, and I released an album, "I Miss You John," to pay tribute to our friend. (Longo titled the album.) In addition to Longo on the piano, others on the album are Frank Wess, James Moody, David Sánchez, tenor sax; Jimmy Owens, Cecil Bridgewater (husband of jazz singer, Dee Dee Bridgewater), trumpet; Paul West, acoustic bass; and Ray Mosca, drums. As with the CDs of Dizzy's South American tour, this CD was produced by Red Anchor Productions and released by Longo's company, Consolidated Artists Productions, Inc.

You don't have to know music to feel the unusual and deep emotion of all the musicians. Upon release of the album, *DownBeat* magazine wrote: "… Expressive sincerity is a gift shared by all the players…"

During one piece, Moody plays a note with such depth that both Longo and I were extremely moved. It sounded like he "spoke" the word "gulermo." It was almost incomprehensible that anyone could produce a note like that. We were in awe, and since then, Longo and I adopted the word to mean "friend," and call each other "my gulermo."

I wrote the following in the liner notes for the "I Miss You John" CD:

"This album, for my part, is dedicated to my dear departed friend who is always with me, no matter what horizon. Not only because of his music, but as a soul who has given so much in just being himself. Those of us who know you are passing your good virtues on — we miss you, John Birks 'Dizzy' Gillespie."

Dizzy's death was an immeasurable loss to the world of music in general and the world of jazz in particular. He was the kind of talent that comes along once in a lifetime. He left an indelible mark on generations of musicians, and I believe that his music will continue to influence artists for many more years. I believe the world still hasn't fully appreciated the full extent of his talents and contributions to jazz. Someday, history will recognize Dizzy as it has the Beethovens and Mozarts.

Yes, other jazz artists like Charlie "Bird" Parker, made contributions to jazz and left their mark. I don't want to take anything away from any of them. Yet, in my opinion, Dizzy's work had just a little more depth, moved the soul just a bit more, and was looked on by jazz aficionados with a little more appreciation. Those playing for and with him, exceptional musicians themselves, stood in awe of him. They knew he was "the master" and were honored to share the world's stages with him.

Let me emphasize that Bird and Dizzy were close friends, bound together by equal talent. They respected each other immensely, and came to each other's defense against critics. Although Bird may have received a little more credit for creating bebop, as I have indicated earlier in this book, Dizzy did not mind. In one interview, Dizzy discussed his relationship with Bird, stating, "No one could have been any closer than Parker and me. We were two peas in a pod...we had the same heartbeat.

"There were people at the time that would try to put a wedge between Charlie Parker...and me. They would come up to me and say 'Parker is the one who invented bebop.' And I would say, 'So he was. What's the difference?'"

Another time, Dizzy told Nat Hentoff, the acclaimed jazz critic, during an interview that Parker's talent was in "phrasing" and "bluesiness." Parker played the blues better "than anybody," Dizzy maintained, concluding, "He [Parker] is the most fantastic musician I ever met."

And it was not just the innovation of bebop which made Dizzy and Bird so special. It was their originality, their unique style and complexity that made them such geniuses.

The music world mourned Dizzy's death, and I grieved because I had lost a brother. I don't want to overuse that word but it was true. He was a part of my family, as close as any other of my relatives. To my kids, when Dizzy visited our home, it was always, "Uncle Dizzy" and they used "uncle" in the true meaning of the word.

We shared in each other's joys and shed tears together when we suffered tragedies. He would be the first one I called when I had problems, whether it involved my family or my business. We shared everything; we had no secrets from each other. He was a part of me.

Let me stress, there was more, much more, to John Birks "Dizzy" Gillespie than his musical talent. All the public ever saw was a highly talented trumpet player who was somewhat of a clown on stage. That stage persona hid the true character of a man who had a high standard of integrity, honesty, and values.

I have already mentioned how he cried when I angrily accused him of undermining our friendship by recording with another label while we were partners in Dee Gee. He recognized his mistake and it shamed him.

I wrote about how, when he traveled to foreign countries, he refused to perform when he learned that poor children, who wanted to attend, were barred from his performances because they couldn't afford the tickets.

I read articles and books that talk about how he refused to be coached when the State Department wanted to brief him on how to answer questions about the U.S. during interviews. He said he would answer forthrightly and honestly. He did not need anyone to tell him what to say. I was not there when he rejected the State Department's offer to brief him but, knowing the man, I believe that the story is credible. Dizzy would always insist on "telling it like it is."

One incident that was so revealing about Dizzy's heart and depth as a human being involved Paul Robeson, singer, actor, and Civil Rights activist who was ostracized in the U.S. because he allegedly was a "Communist sympathizer" at a time when Americans were in panic about "the Red scare."

The story began when I was nine years old. I was in the Glee Club at the Roosevelt Elementary School and heard a song, "Ballad for Americans," which Robeson recorded in 1939. The music was composed by Earl Robinson, and the lyrics were written by John LaTouche. I was enthralled by this highly patriotic song which spoke of American values. I never forgot the opening of the song:

> *In seventy-six the sky was red*
> *Thunder rumbling overhead*
> *Bad King George couldn't sleep in his bed*
> *And on that stormy morn, Ol' Uncle Sam was born.*
> *Some birthday!*

The lyrics addressed this country's diversity, values, and tolerance for different races and religions, and included the following verse:

> *A man in white skin can never be free while his black brother is in slavery.*
> *"And we here highly resolve that these dead shall not have died in vain.*
> *And this government of the people, by the people, and for the people*
> *Shall not perish from the Earth."*
> *Abraham Lincoln said that on November 19,*
> *1863 at Gettysburg, Pennsylvania.*

I asked the Glee Club music teacher, Mrs. Margaret Brown, whether the club could perform the song, but she replied that the school did not have the sheet music or the funds to buy it. I went to the Jewish Center on Woodward and Holbrook in Detroit, where I was a volunteer on the center's newspaper. I raised some money which I used to buy the sheet music at Grinnell Brothers Music House near downtown Detroit. The music teacher was elated and had us perform the song — it was 12 minutes and 45 seconds long . We sang it with all of the club's members wearing costumes representing different eras in America's history.

Robeson had made the song famous and years later, I asked Dizzy if he would do a version of the piece, and he agreed to the project. The problem was: How would we finance the production? At the time, we needed the funds. We decided to approach the PR executive of a major oil company for the needed financial support. We were turned down. Neither Dizzy nor I knew exactly why, but we assumed because Robeson was so closely identified with the song and because he was persona non grata in the U.S, the company did not want to be associated with the proposed recording. We did not try anywhere else, concluding that the reaction would be the same at other corporations or non-profit funding organizations. Robeson was an untouchable. So we dropped plans for the project entirely. But, as I write this book, I am still planning to restore that project. My passion for this song has never ebbed.

Dizzy's respect and admiration for Robeson were all too evident one day when Dizzy was playing at the Apollo Theater in Harlem and Robeson walked into his dressing room. Dizzy, who had known Robeson, was stunned, and as they were exchanging greetings, the stagehands shouted "it's the half," meaning the performers had a half-hour before it was time to appear on stage.

Upon hearing the alert, Robeson said to Dizzy, "I gotta go…I don't want anyone to see you with me." That just about broke Dizzy's heart, and he sat in his dressing room crying his ass off. Dizzy despised discrimination of any kind, and he felt helpless as Robeson walked out of the room. Regrettably, there was nothing he could do for Robeson.

Dizzy was in awe of Robeson, stating that the singer/actor/activist was a forerunner to Dr. Martin Luther King, Jr. Dizzy said the following about Robeson in his autobiography:

"The dues that Paul Robeson paid were worse than the dues Martin Luther King paid. Martin Luther only paid (with) his life, quick, for his views, but Paul Robeson had to suffer a very long time.

"I dug Paul Robeson right away, from the first words. A lot of black people were against Paul Robeson; he was trying to help them and they were talking against him, like he was a communist. I heard him speak on many occasions and, man, talk about a speaker. He could really speak. And he was fearless! You never hear people speak out like he did with everything arrayed against you, and come out like he did. Man, I'll remember Paul Robeson until I die. He was something else. Paul Robeson became 'Mr. Incorruptible.' No one could get to him because that's the rarest quality in man, incorruptibility."

Of all the awards Dizzy won, he treasured the Paul Robeson Award (from the Rutgers University Institute for Jazz Studies) perhaps the most. Dizzy stated unabashedly in his book that the Robeson award "...gave me the greatest sense of pride."

Discussing the award to Dizzy, Christopher White, the Institute's director, said: "...it became obvious to me that it was necessary to institute an award that would be given to people who, themselves, were other manifestations of the African continuum in this American milieu. Without a doubt, Dizzy, to my way of thinking, was the epitome of that, given African-American music."

Dizzy tried to help whenever he was able to. As he was being treated for pancreatic cancer at Englewood Hospital and Medical Center in Englewood, New Jersey, where Dizzy and his wife lived, he expressed two wishes: to assure continued support for jazz and jazz musicians; and to have a memorial in his name at Englewood.

Dizzy offered to let the hospital use his name, and perhaps that would help in raising funds to assist needy musicians. Thus, the Dizzy Gillespie Memorial Fund was created to underwrite diagnostic tests, and surgical and medical care for jazz musicians who were uninsured and didn't have the ability to pay medical costs. The fund was supported by Lorraine and other relatives and friends of Dizzy. In partnership with the New York City-based Jazz Foundation of America, a network of more than 50 doctors in a variety of specialties offers free care to musicians at the hospital. At the time of this writing, the fund had provided more than $5 million for a broad range of medical services.

The hospital also created "Dizzy's Corner" in the lobby of the hospital where jazz musicians play every Wednesday for visitors and patients. The musicians huddle around a piano and jam. The hospital has reserved the "Corner" for Wednesdays, but many jazz artists play on other days as well. I am sure these sessions put a smile on Dizzy's face.

As I reflect in this book on my life with Dizzy for almost 50 years, I realize again that I had a unique and rewarding experience. I witnessed the development of the best jazz, including bebop, in the history of music. That music, as Annie Ross sang, is forever as are Dizzy's spirit as a musician and his reputation as a man who lived by the highest values.

Who can ask for anything more? I know I can't.

So, to you Diz, later, bro'.

LEGACY

16

What is Dizzy's legacy? At this writing, it has been more than 20 years since he passed away, and I believe that question will be examined, analyzed and debated for generations to come.

Much has been written about his contributions. There were so many dimensions to Dizzy's talent that scholars and musicians will study his work for decades. I believe a major part of Dizzy's genius was his willingness and ability to innovate, even if, at times, it was off-beat (no pun intended) and unorthodox. For instance, for years, Dizzy collaborated with a talented arranger, Gil Fuller, who also had worked for Benny Carter, Woody Herman, Count Basie, and other famous musicians. At times, for Dizzy's musical productions, Fuller used the so-called Schillinger System of Music Composition which, in brief, relies on mathematical processes. It was developed by Joseph Schillinger, a Russian mathematician. Innovation and experimentation were among Dizzy's hallmarks.

I thought the best way to end this book would be to quote some jazz experts who knew him best. Below, I quote some of his contemporaries, world-class musicians and jazz experts. These comments were made in different venues, and they are sentiments which I found particularly moving, and which I thought were unusually insightful.

Phil Woods, alto sax:*

"That's the most important musician to ever come out of jazz because...he had it all...He was always modest, humble about his contributions...Dizzy was the guy who took it all and carried it to the end...he was always going to school...he was a student all his life...when you got the rhythm that Birks had, plus the harmonic sophistication that he had, that's the whole package..."

"Man, when he takes the batting stance and puts that horn up to his chops...he hits it out of the park...It's gonna take a hundred years to sort it out (Dizzy's talent)...the cats will always know it...people had a funny viewpoint of who this Dizzy was...that crazy guy, that funny guy...they had no idea of his depth..."

Lalo Schifrin, composer, pianist and conductor:*

"When I heard Dizzy for the first time, I was knocked out... it was like a religious conversion...I was 16 years old...in Buenos Aires..."

"Many years later, I told an audience, I have had many teachers but only one master — Dizzy Gillespie...he taught me many, many things...When he died, I said that perhaps the intricate lines that Dizzy played, the angular and asymmetrical lines that he played, perhaps they were a message of God that was up to us to decipher.

"He had a conception of music which was very unusual. I hate to say the word revolutionary, but he was a revolutionary not in the sense of negation of the past. Dizzy did not negate the past. He extended it; it was an extension of the past. In that sense, he became a big influence for everybody. People should understand the importance that Dizzy Gillespie had in the history of jazz but also on music of the 20th century..."

---

*In interviews with me on CDs of the 1956 U.S. State Department tour of South America.

Donald L. Maggin, author of a biography on Dizzy, and producer of jazz concerts:*

"He was a great artist, a self-taught trumpet virtuoso...one of the finest improvisers of the 20ᵗʰ century...and the owner of a musical intelligence of the highest order. He vastly enriched this jazz art form by being an organizer, and a tireless recruiter of talent...he was a wonderfully effective teacher and proselytizer for jazz.

"His generosity of spirit and warm infectious openness gladdened everybody who came into contact with him. Dizzy was the creator of the most important and aesthetic revolution in jazz history — bebop — which graphically recast both the rhythmic and harmonic basis of the music."

Jimmy Heath, saxophonist, composer, arranger:*

"Dizzy Gillespie, to me, is my mentor...I loved Dizzy Gillespie's approach to music...he was an entertainer...but he was crazy like a fox as some people wrote back in those days...he was such an intelligent man...he acted comically...like a comic...but he was very serious when he put that horn to his mouth..."

Mike Longo, pianist who played with Dizzy for 24 years:*

"He was a musical prophet...he was to our music what Jesus and Mohammed and Moses were to religion. When he put his horn up to his mouth, he was as serious as a heart attack."

---

*From a panel discussion, "Celebrating Dizzy Gillespie," at Saint Peter's Church in New York, March 12, 2012, 19 years after Dizzy's death.

Stanley Crouch, poet, novelist and jazz critic:*

> "Dizzy Gillespie was a very unusual person because he was such a remarkable musical intellectual...I mean he wasn't on the second floor, he wasn't on the third floor, he wasn't on the fifth floor. Wherever the penthouse of musical intellect was, he had a room up there.

> "One of the most remarkable things about Dizzy was his trumpet style...it was never an easy trumpet style...if we look at the history of jazz trumpeters, nobody has ever played a style that complex and has become successful...I mean successful at the level Dizzy was."

Gary Giddins, *Village Voice* columnist and jazz critic:*

> "He was one of the gods, one of the people who gave us the music. You felt like he was inventing the trumpet. There was so much fun and a sense of excitement that here we were doing something that nobody else on earth could do."

George Benson, guitar:†

> "I don't know who I enjoyed more: Dizzy the man with the most wonderful personality and wit, or the incredible innovator who remained one of the most beloved humans, in or out of the world of music. If Dizzy was as gracious and kind to all he encountered as he was toward me, it isn't hard to understand why he was so loved.

> "Dizzy Gillespie's approach to music was an experience that was rich in lessons of harmony and theory but always felt good. To play with him was to touch greatness."

---

*From a panel discussion, "Celebrating Dizzy Gillespie," at Saint Peter's Church in New York, March 12, 2012, 19 years after Dizzy's death.

†From *Dizzy Gillespie*, a book of photos by Dany Gignoux, Dizzy's official photographer who periodically traveled with him.

Benny Golson, tenor sax:*

"My life had two beginnings: When I was born and when I first heard Dizzy. He changed my life forever with his music. How glad I am that I was born in his time!"

Claudio Roditi, trumpet, flugelhorn:*

"Playing with Dizzy Gillespie for five years made me realize many things about this master. The main one was his total dedication and commitment to his music. He was always looking for new ways to approach a chord progression, different notes to fit a certain chord. He always seemed to be thinking about music. Perhaps the most important lesson I received from him was that to be great one needs full-time commitment to what one wishes to do."

Finally, I think that Alyn Shipton, author of the Dizzy biography, *Groovin' High, The Life of Dizzy Gillespie,* captured the essence of Dizzy's untiring and constant efforts to achieve "world unity" when he wrote:

"From the ideal platform of his United Nation Orchestra, with its pathbreaking fusion of musical styles from North, Central, and South America, and the Caribbean, he had demonstrated the commitment to the principles of unity, peace, and brotherhood of which he spoke so often. He ended his autobiography with the wish that he would be remembered as a humanitarian."

I think Dizzy has been granted his wish. Yes, generations will continue to marvel at his musical skills, but they will also honor John Birks "Dizzy" Gillespie for his commitment to mankind.

---

*From *Dizzy Gillespie*, a book of photos by Dany Gignoux, Dizzy's official photographer who periodically traveled with him.

Postscript

I'm so lucky to be a jazz musician.

John Birks "Dizzy" Gillespie

Acknowledgments

In writing this book, I had only one objective which was to capture and save some treasured stories about a professional and personal partnership I had with one of music's all-time greats which I thought jazz and other music lovers and the general public would enjoy.

I wrote in some liner notes years ago, "History in music, like in all other disciplines, needs to be served." I hope I served it well. I also hope that memory has served me well. If I have made any mistakes, I regret them and apologize, particularly if I offended anyone.

Berl and I want to thank and express our appreciation to several people and institutions who helped confirm facts and details while complementing my recollections with important information. They include (in alphabetical order):

Ramona Crowell, Dizzy's running mate when Dizzy announced his candidacy for president in 1964.

Donald Epstein, of Vesco Corp.

Charlie Fishman, Dizzy's personal manager and producer for many years.

Marion "Boo" Frazier, Dizzy's cousin who was in charge of logistics in the 1956 tour of South America.

Charlie "Whale" Lake, Dizzy's tour manager for 18 years.

Mike Longo, pianist for Dizzy for 24 years.

David C. Miller, Jr., special assistant for National Security Affairs for President George H.W. Bush.

Lynne Mueller, of New York's Saint Peter's Church.

Edward Nykiel, grandson of the man who constructed the building I would buy to house my company, Marine Pollution Control.

Lalo Schifrin, world-renowned composer, arranger and conductor.

Sergeant Scot Sowden, of the Wilmington, Delaware Police Department.

Patricia Willard, Southern California campaign chairperson in the 1964 "Dizzy Gillespie for President" campaign.

Dr. Clyde Wu, a member of the Detroit Symphony Orchestra Board of Directors.

Al Young, novelist, poet, and State of California poet laureate emeritus.

We extend our appreciation to officials at the Carter and Clinton presidential libraries, the Englewood Hospital and Medical Center in Englewood, New Jersey, the Kennedy Center for the Performing Arts in Washington, D.C, the Detroit Symphony Orchestra in Detroit, Michigan, and the Bahá'í Centers in New York City, Eloy, Arizona, and Evanston, Illinois.

In addition, we want to indicate that frequently we consulted Dizzy's autobiography and several biographies on Dizzy to confirm facts and flesh out events that we refer to in this book. We are indebted to the authors, and their books are listed in the bibliography at the back of this book.

Of course, we want to express our gratitude to Nat Hentoff, Alyn Shipton and Doug Ramsey for their very kind and gracious remarks on the back cover. We are flattered by their comments and very appreciative.

Dave Usher

Additional Acknowledgments

I want to especially thank my grandchildren for assisting with the index, a tedious but vital and important part of this project. It takes patience, intelligence, and dedication, and my three grandchildren, Jackie, Erik and Alex, have these qualities in abundance. At the time they developed the index in 2014, they were 14, 12, and 12 respectively.

I want to acknowledge my sister-in-law, Debbie Zager, for her editing of this book. This is the second time I have been the beneficiary of her exceptional talents and both books have been the better for it.

My thanks also go to Ann BeVier, the mother of my son-in-law, Peter. Like Debbie, Ann has given me her editing advice for the second time, and I am indebted to her once more.

Finally, my wife, Phyllis, put her keen editing skills to the manuscript and, as always, made invaluable contributions. Through the years, she has edited all my books and articles, and her advice made my work so much better. Her most valuable contribution has been the "editing" of my life for more than 52 years to make it more fulfilling.

Berl Falbaum

About the Authors

Dave Usher: He has had two very different careers. In one, he produced records and CDs, working not just with Dizzy Gillespie, his life-long friend, but also with some of the world's greatest jazz musicians. In the other, he was a pioneer in developing sophisticated techniques and methods to clean up oil spills and hazardous materials. In 1967, he founded Detroit's Marine Pollution Control (MPC), an internationally renowned environmental services company, the first such company in the Great Lakes region and one of the first in the U.S. Usher appointed Dizzy to MPC's Board of Directors. Usher also helped establish the American Salvage Association (ASA), and he was the founder of the Oil Spill Control Association of America (OSCAA) which later changed its name to the Spill Control Association of America (SCAA), and the International Spill Control Organization (ISCO.) In addition to helping establish these organizations, he served as president of OSCAA, SCAA, ISCO and the Hazardous Materials Control Research Institute (HMCRI) for many years.

Berl Falbaum: His career includes ten years as a political reporter for *The Detroit News*, fifteen years in corporate public relations and four years in state politics as administrative aide to Michigan's lieutenant governor. He founded his own PR company, Falbaum & Associates, in 1989. He has published seven other books and taught journalism part-time for 45 years at Wayne State University in Detroit. He also wrote one play which was produced by a community theatre in Livonia, Michigan. His articles on politics and the media appear frequently on the Op-Ed pages of Michigan's newspapers. He lives with his wife, Phyllis, in West Bloomfield, Michigan. They have two daughters and three grandchildren.

His other books include: *Just for Fun, The Anchor, Leo & Friends, A Matter of Precedents, The Definitive Guide to Organizational Backstabbing, The Definitive Guide to Organizational Backstabbing Volume II, Shanghai Remembered,* and *Prince of Omertá* (with Giovanni Gambino.)

Bibliography

Cohodas, Nadine, *Spinning Blues into Gold: The Chess Brothers and the Legendary Chess Records*, New York: St. Martin's Press, 2000.

Gignoux, Dany, *Dizzy Gillespie*, Kiel, Germany: Nieswand Verlag, 1993.

Gillespie, Dizzy with Al Fraser, *To Be, or Not...To Bop: Dizzy Gillespie*, London: W.H. Allen & Company, Ltd., 1980.

Grouse, Leslie, *Dizzy Gillespie and the Birth of Bebop*, New York: Atheneum, Macmillan Publishing Company, 1994.

Kofsky, Frank, *Black Music, White Business: Illuminating the History and Political Economy of Jazz*, New York: Pathfinder Press, 1998.

Maggin, Donald L., *The Life and Times of Dizzy Gillespie*, New York: HarperCollins Publishers Inc., 2005.

Shipton, Alyn, *Groovin' High, The Life of Dizzy Gillespie*, Oxford, New York: Oxford University Press, 1999.

Index

Epstein, Eugene, 14

Epstein, Nathan, 14

Epstein, Richard, 14

Europe, 24, 83, 109, 126, 127

Evans, Gil, 107

"Extensions," 74

Exxon Valdez, 50

Ezeiza Airport, 59

F

Facio, Joe, 30

Fairfax, Frankie, 29

Falbaum, Berl, i, ix, 49, 86, 126, 128, 137

Farragut, David Glasgow, 17, 18

Faubus, Orval, E., Arkansas Governor, 70

Fields, Kansas, 39

Fiore, Nick, 82

Fisher, Max M., 14

Fisher, William, 14

Fishman, Charlie, 104, 126-128, 132, 137, 138

Fitzgerald, Ella, 8, 94

Five Scalders (The), 45

Flax, Marty, 58

Flushing Cemetery, 139

"For Love of Country: The Arturo Sandoval Story," 128

Ford Motor Co. Rouge Plant, 12, 48

Fournier, Vernell, 74

France, 16, 25, 118, 140

Franklin D. Roosevelt School, 65

Fraser, Al, 29

Frazier, Marion "Boo," 67, 73

Fresedo, Osvaldo, 64, 65, 68

Friedman, Martin, 116

Frohnmayer, John E., 116

Fuller, Walter Gilbert "Gil," 148

G

Gabrilowitsch, Ossip Salomonowitsch, 3

Gafa, Al, 96

Galpin, Richard, Dr., 82

Gant, Frank, 78

Gar Wood, 49

Geer, Bill, 7

Geinbog, Hage, 133

Geodesic Dome, 82

Georgia, 111

Gerdine, Leigh, 116

Gettysburg, Pennsylvania, 143

Getz, Stan, 107

Giddins, Gary, 151

Gignoux, Dany, 121, 123, 151, 152

"Gillespiana Suite," 63

Gillespie, John Birks "Dizzy," ii-iv, vii-ix, 1, 2, 6-9, 22-27, 51, 71, 73, 76, 78, 79, 153; nickname, trumpet, cheeks, 28-33; Dee Gee, 34-43; tours S. America, 1956, 52-68; runs for president, 80-90; race, 91-99; Bahá'í Faith, 100-105;

www.ingramcontent.com/pod-product-compliance
Lightning Source LLC
Chambersburg PA
CBHW052043090426
42739CB00010B/2024